When the Dust Settles

LUCY EASTHOPE

When the Dust Settles

Searching for Hope After Disaster

HODDER

First published in Great Britain in 2022 by Hodder & Stoughton
An Hachette UK company

This paperback edition published in 2023

2

Copyright © Lucy Easthope 2022

A CIP catalogue record for this title is available from the British Library

Paperback ISBN 9781529358285
eBook ISBN 9781529358261

Typeset in Plantin Light by Hewer Text UK Ltd, Edinburgh
Printed and bound in Great Britain by Clays Ltd, Elcograf S.p.A.

Hodder & Stoughton policy is to use papers that are natural, renewable
and recyclable products and made from wood grown in sustainable
forests. The logging and manufacturing processes are expected to
conform to the environmental regulations of the country of origin.

Hodder & Stoughton Ltd
Carmelite House
50 Victoria Embankment
London EC4Y 0DZ

www.hodder.co.uk

This book is dedicated to those who lost their lives in the events described within its pages, and the people who loved them.

Contents

PROLOGUE
Arrival

It's raining hard. Water trails down the windscreen and the wipers squeal with the effort. I can't drive, so have earned a reputation for getting as close to the cordon tape as possible in a taxi. I have grown to trust just one driver, Jay. He has taken me to locations all around the country and sometimes to airports or train stations in the middle of the night.

I have honed my rituals over a decade. I play Eminem on my iPod. I use the beat to get up the necessary resolve for what is about to come and to separate the world I've left from the one I'm about to enter. Sometimes I fall asleep and Jay turns up the radio to drown out my snoring. I know he will give me a ten-minute warning when he thinks we are close. He can't always be sure that we are there yet because there are no signposts to a new disaster. There will be small cues though: a police car and the van of a Tactical Support Unit. A welfare truck supplied by the fire service. A fleet of private ambulances.

Eventually, we pull up at a kerb and I peel out of the back with my rucksack and wheelie bag, feeling like a chubby air hostess. I pull up my coat hood, cursing. I know the rain will threaten the forensic integrity of the scene, as it forms a soup with the mud and the kerosene and the blood. It will also make the responders impatient and irritable. I gather my breath and breathe in, deep from the diaphragm like the psychologist who tended to the fire crews at the Oklahoma City bombings taught me. Then, I look for the doorway to hell.

I'm always struck by how fine the line between catastrophe and the rest of the world can be. Here it is mere metres. Motorway traffic roars close enough to lift the hair on my fringe. One of the very first items on an emergency responder checklist is the securing of the scene and so a fence is up and already fraying. The chunky metal is shrouded in flapping thick white plastic and green canvas, shielding the disaster within from prying eyes and unwelcome visitors. The fences can't keep out the newest way to sneak a look, however, and, despite the weather, there is a constant buzz of drones owned by the news organisations. The chief constable is working on some sort of drone exclusion zone but the additional legislation to control and seize them is years away.

If you get there early enough, police might still be guarding the entrance points. Usually it's the youngest of the crew – senior officers deliberately select the newer recruits to toughen them up. But there have been budget cuts again and it is now five days after the incident occurred, so this time it's a private security guard: mouth set to mute, identification badge front and centre, bomber jacket, angry stubble. I recognise something in his face as he looks at me. He has been told to expect me but I am not what he pictured. I am a short woman, rounded by years of trying (and failing) to make babies. Arthritis has hobbled my gait to give me a rolling walk. I am clumsy. I am northern. No Bond movie would have cast me. I smile broadly at him. You learn early on that you can't show fear or weakness. The cards are stacked against you already for not being police or forensics. And for being a woman. So, you perfect your swagger.

I sign the log. I breathe in again. I am in.

A small plane has crashed into the road, ploughing into a series of cars and spectators. A crane is being readied to lift twisted sheets of plane wing. I know that at least eleven people have died and several more are injured. I am looking at a landscape where bent metal has fused with herbage, body parts and shoes, over several miles. The aftermath of an air crash can defy the physics of how people should fit together and also mess with the rules of topography in the area where they land. Aircraft pilots are trained to try to aim their failing planes at scrubland or an empty park, so before the world lands on them these are often the most mundane of places. Last week, this was just a verge of knotted thistles and thorns, a decade of Evian bottles and Walkers crisps wrappers sewn into the scrubland, with a series of broken registration plates marking the scenes of historic fender benders. Now, it is a Bosch's *Garden of Earthly Delights* for the modern time. Paramedics' detritus marks out the location of attempts to attend to the sole survivor, who is now fighting for his life in the local hospital. Wads of cloth, gauze and tubing float on the surface of a large puddle. I notice a thermos flask and the twisted limbs of a camping chair strewn nearby. Objects, dents and marks all put on their own little mystery play.

I try to stay both out of the way and upright, avoiding pools of kerosene, thistles and a reversing incident welfare unit. The 'blue light' responders – police, fire and ambulance personnel – have long gone. Now it is the turn of the investigators, detectives and body recovery officers. I watch as a policewoman bags up a crisp packet and some leaves from a bush to be sent off for DNA testing, in case it's all the confirmation we can get. The recovery of the bodies, or, more accurately, the body parts, takes days, which is always too long for waiting families. Bones and teeth can take weeks to emerge from wreckage and soil.

I stand and I look. This long after the initial crash and most of what was a recognisable body part has been removed but the smaller fragments remain. The violence that has occurred here is breathtaking. Kinetic forces acting on an aircraft are brutal to flesh and bone; the top-heavy head on the frame of a bi-ped is ripe for decapitation. I never shy away from what I see. My coping mechanism has been to unpick what I am looking at; at a scene, and more often at the mortuary I find myself intensely studying the *once-a-person* over and over to try to work out what went where. I move my head from side to side to try to decipher what was a personal item from someone's pocket and what was plane upholstery or metalwork, both now embedding in the soft, human frame.

There is always the fantasy plan and then the reality. We train for clement conditions and for an organised, measured response with time to make decisions. One of the fantasies of body recovery at a scene like this is that there will be time to carefully place each body fragment into a plastic bag that is then carefully labelled with a sticky barcode. But so often there isn't time. Here, the rain has seen to that. Forensic scientists are getting soaked as they scrutinise the scene and one of them eyes me and my now sodden wheelie bag sceptically.

I know what he's thinking. What the fuck am I doing there?

I'm what comes next. I am one of the country's top advisers on disaster recovery. I am called in to size up the scale of what is to be faced and what can be done about it. Police and local responders might only see a major incident like this once in their career but I have seen them over and over again: nuclear incidents, chemical attacks, pandemics, food shortages, fuel shortages, trains and plane crashes, volcanoes and tsunamis. Companies, governments, countries all have to be prepared for catastrophe. Few people know that planning like this exists but disaster specialists can be found all over the place if you know where to look – town halls, fire and rescue and police services, NHS trusts, universities, airlines and cruise companies. We are a Cinderella service, sweeping up below stairs. Some of us are independent contractors; others work for private disaster management companies. Collectively, we are a giant Elastoplast for when the worst happens.

There are two main aspects of our profession: writing the emergency plans, so that people have a map to follow when the worst happens, and responding, following in the wake of disaster to set the pathway for recovery. The work of UK disaster response is multi-faceted. We help to run investigations, build mortuaries and oversee identification, burials, personal effects and repatriations. I have learned to plan and to respond with all the others. But I have also developed my own niche in addressing what comes later still. For the recovery as well as the response. I try to take the affected community a step further and ask what they need in order to face a post-disaster future with assurance. Often the recovery needs very different resources, and approaches, than the response. I have been all around the world to study what works and what heaps further harms onto the initial disaster.

I have worked in emergency response and planning for two decades now, advising ministers, governments, private clients, archbishops and the military. But I always wait to be invited in. My job is to see the whole picture of the disaster aftermath. Not just the next few hours, days or weeks, but months and years. I often arrive after the first stage of the response work is done, when the fire and ambulance services are packing up their kit and moving on. The initial adrenaline rush of the emergency is over quickly but disaster recovery is the long game – 'not the sprint, not even a marathon, more like the worst kind of endurance event imaginable'.[1]

Then, somewhat perversely, I use everything I've learned to get us better prepared for the next disaster. That part of my profession is called 'emergency planning'. I write what are known as emergency plans for the government as well as for all sorts of organisations. We write them before an incident happens and then test them until they are needed. They are how we try to bring order to the messy realities of life during and after disaster. The moments, hours and days after a flood, a fire at a care home, a bomb blast in an aircraft hold, are febrile and chaotic. Events occur outside any sort of linear, controlled structure and present those confronted by them with the task of *doing something*. The plan is supposed to make those moments more manageable for emergency responders and a whole raft of other organisations. So, I'm what comes next but I'm also what came before because I wrote the plan.

I know every major incident that the UK and its citizens have endured overseas since 1960 inside and out and have worked, in some way, on the response to every single one since 2001. You might think I'd lose count but I don't because each disaster is seared into my brain and has nudged and shaped every aspect of my life and my very self. The Indian Ocean tsunami, 9/11, the Bali bombings, the 7/7 attacks, Grenfell Tower.[2] There are some where only a few really understand how close we came to global carnage: the

Japanese tsunami and concurrent nuclear disaster of 2011. And there are the 'quieter' ones. The poisoning of former Russian agents in London and then, a decade later, Salisbury. The carefully planned raids on factories full of trafficked human slaves, the floods, the shootings, the fires. And, then of course, the latest: the global Covid-19 pandemic, which, contrary to some myths, was the most diligently planned-for risk in British history.

The poet W. H. Auden wrote in 1936 about how, in one part of a place, a tragedy of the most unimaginable horror can be unfolding; a family's life can be devastated. While in another part of the same panorama, a farmer can continue to plough his field, someone else is eating 'or just walking dully along'. People who have somewhere to go sail calmly on. Life simply goes on all around the suffering.

I have made my life around walking towards the unfolding disaster and I am by no means the only one: we are a whole profession dedicated to cleaning up after the worst has happened. We perform an important service but also a hidden one, and I wanted to write a book that might bring what we do into the light. Disaster exposes us, our society, and our leaders, to our core. This is a book about catastrophic events and frail bodies and loss and bereavement. But it is also a book about hope and revival and laughter. Friendship, resilience and love.

My role adapts depending on what each disaster requires. At this particular crash scene, I am here to advise the coroner, who is the chair of a hurriedly formed Mass Fatalities Co-ordinating Group (MFCG). When I see a disaster unfold, my first thought is of the needs of the dead, of the grieving and of those who care for both. The MFCG is the place where the local responders bring together the key people tasked with caring for the dead as soon as possible after the incident. It is an innovation I pushed for during the mid-2000s, as it had become obvious that the myriad issues that come with caring for the deceased and the bereaved can easily get lost in the response-focused Strategic Co-ordinating Group (SCG).

This SCG meeting – also known as 'Gold' to signify that the highest level of leaders attend (it should be said loudly in the style of the Spandau Ballet pop hit) – is where emergency response is at its most thrusty: emergency responders aping military generals and yessing or noing on things that will save or destroy, from a location often many miles away from the incident scene. The dead and the newly bereaved can get forgotten. The MFCG is a way to keep a necessary focus on them. It is theoretically given the same status but those protecting the dead of disaster often have to fight hard to be heard.

At this scene, as with all of them, I tread carefully, both literally and metaphorically. It is my job to join the dots between this and other recent disasters and to point out the bear traps these teams cannot see. I recognise a large police inspector, Steve, who heads over with a nod and a warm smile. I ask after his two daughters and son, who I know are his world. 'Tricky one, this, Luce,' he says and we swap some whispered notes on our worries so far – the bear traps, the personalities and the political and legal 'challenges' that are already emerging. He also tips me off about where advice will and won't be welcome. Some of their equipment requests have already been turned down.

Steve leads me over to the exhibits tent. A savage gorse bush catches my trousers and rips off a large piece of cloth as I go. I pick it off to make sure it doesn't get bundled up with the evidence. Inside, another officer is labelling and inventorying hundreds of items. I step in as he is inspecting a battered wallet. He views me suspiciously until Steve introduces me as 'one of the gang'. Steve and I watch as he strains the leather of each fold of the wallet to make sure he has extracted everything, including a few coins and some fluff, before noting them down. Inside one of the folds is a scrunched up notelet with a child's cartoon character embossed on it. Large, loopy hand-writing from small child to Dad.

How to deal with and process the overwhelming amount of precious personal effects from the dead is one of the things I am most frequently asked to help with. I advise on their storage and care and emphasise that nothing should be thrown away until the family have been asked what they want, because that mistake is irreversible. Decisions like these, made in the early stages of a disaster, while the smoke still hangs heavy in the air, can later reap their own secondary disaster on the lost and the living.

In the midst of chaos, we make decisions hot and fast, falling back on bad habits to buy ourselves time. Log entries get missed out and are occasionally even changed after the fact. We make assumptions and therefore mistakes. I shudder when someone nearby uses the term accident. 'Accident' is not a benign term. Because even starting to think that something *might* have been an accident can mean we leave other trails to go cold. Painful experience has taught me that the person in the driver's seat was not necessarily the driver. An air crash is not always pilot error. In those first few chaotic hours it is tempting to make things 'simpler', to record a blanket time of death for each deceased rather than the individual circumstances of each demise. But in disasters there are many ways to die and over so many minutes, and every family is entitled to their own story. Until you have faced such a loss you cannot know what strange comfort small details like this can bring.

Meanwhile, the recovered body parts have been moved to a refrigerated unit and then transported to the mortuary that has been readied some miles away. 'Normal business' (other bodies) has been hastily relocated to another city and this mortuary will now be dedicated to this disaster's dead and the many challenges they will bring. I catch a lift with a stocky young officer who I met on a course in Northern Ireland a couple of years previously. In the car, we talk like normal people, about her kids and the rain and how everybody has managed to rip their standard issue trousers. She tells me the senior officer has forgotten to sign off the new trousers order and we chuckle about the possibility of no one having trousers. One of the shiny, black 'private ambulances' transporting the remains pulls out in front of us on the motorway and I catch a glimpse of blacked-out windows. As a child, I used to think private ambulances were cars rich people paid for to get to hospital in style, kitted out inside like the limo that took me to my sixth-form prom. But now I know these are funeral directors' vehicles, with racking in the back that secure trays of black-bagged bodies.[3]

We slip into the mortuary as the scenes of crime photographers squash around the latest body parts as they are assembled on the gurney – a metal table with a drain at one end. The coroner has asked for me to spot anything wrong or amiss. Unintentional harms that might be done to the deceased or their families. I am there as a pair of eyes on her behalf, to ensure that the processes we rely on are working as they should. Later, she will drive me to the hotel and I will debrief her en route. I shall deliver the 'shit sandwich' – two pieces of good news, wrapped around something that she might need to watch for in the middle.

Around me, I see lots of familiar faces – the pathologist, with whom I have worked on several incidents, a mortuary manager from a training session I ran a year before, a couple of anatomical pathology technologists and an anthropologist. We share smiles and promises of a catch up later on. When the bodies are present, at both scene and mortuary, the dialogue is clipped and functional. The anecdotes and laughter are saved for afterwards. There are two worlds and as soon as you step into one you leave the other behind, even mid-sentence.

I know some of these men and women well, from working in the thick of disaster aftermath and from the debriefing in the bar afterwards. Some of these pairs of hands have literally held me up or pushed me to sit down, hidden me from view, fed me Haribo, or pushed two paracetamol and a bottle of water under the door of a grimy toilet cubicle. The ground for these relationships has been laid in the bleakest of times, which has helped them to endure – even much later on in my career, when things became more difficult. Although the price you pay for belonging to this tribe is separation from the rest of the world and even from your own family.

It is late when we finish at the mortuary and the police have found me a spare room at a local motel. A quiet word with the manager means that a dimly lit corner of the bar will be kept open for the motley disaster response crew – police officers, forensics and me. The police logistics teams know to try to book motels far from the hotels being hastily booked for the families, and by the news organisations, and so we can relax a little here, share stories, even laugh. I know I will be back here tomorrow night and returning to the mortuary for the next few months at least. I know that next week I may be asked to speak to a police exhibits team, to the hastily appointed government minister and, hardest of all, a wide-eyed, sleep-deprived group of bereaved relatives. And I know I will find it impossible to tell the man I love what I have seen. The words stopped forming on my palate a long time ago.

Any soldier or scientist, disaster worker or United Nations war crimes investigator who heads off on deployment will tell you that 'demobbing' is the toughest part. Trying to fit back into your family roles again. Refocusing your brain on small talk and a grocery list. Steadying your nerves when you reach for a household object – a toothbrush, a pen – the brand that you've seen in the wreckage.

The hardest part of working in disaster is going home.

I

The Planner

I think I have always been aware of the sliver of difference between near miss and tragedy.

In the winter of 1978, my mum visited a locum General Practitioner with the symptoms of a urinary tract infection. She remembers him being dismissive and uninterested, as he lazily prescribed an antibiotic, which she dutifully took. It was contraindicated in pregnancy.

The placenta abrupted and a premature labour began. She was rushed to hospital. Soon after, I was delivered by emergency caesarean section, via a rushed vertical incision. Like the three little goat kids cut from the wolf. My dad begged them to save my mum as he was bustled out of the room and she bled out all over the floor. My mum was transfused for several hours and close to death for a week.

It was an early experience for my family of how wrong things can go in no time at all. A lesson in the severe consequences of events that are preventable. Perhaps it's just the bias of hindsight but some of my earliest memories are of being aware of risks in a different way to other people, feeling them as tangible and imminent. In my family, the story is that I was born that way.

I am a child of the indomitable city of Liverpool, where tragedy and activism is wired into the blood. In 1939 my grandad, 'Oohie Jack', watched helplessly from Liverpool Bay as the HMS *Thetis* submarine sank, slowly suffocating the ninety-nine men on board – one in a long line of defining tragedies that have befallen the cities on either side of the Mersey river, in addition to the socio-economic and political battering that peaked in the 1980s. Although it was a decade before my dad was even born, the slow drowning of the *Thetis* submarine loomed large in our imaginations and was a topic of childhood fascination for me.

I passed by my first disaster scene when I was eight years old. My parents were teachers who spent swathes of their career wrangling in secondary schools in the deprived, inner-city areas of Toxteth, Walton and Tuebrook. In March 1987, my mum had arranged a school trip to visit West Germany and we all went along for the ride. My parents, my five-year-old little sister and I were all sailing on the sister ferry of the ill-fated *Herald of Free Enterprise*. As we approached the place in the Channel where 193 passengers and 38 crew members had lost their lives and hundreds of others had scrambled out into the waters, we stood on the decks in silence.

Herald of Free Enterprise had capsized two weeks earlier, on 6 March 1987, outside the harbour of Zeebrugge. She was still there, on her side and partially submerged, when we passed by. My strongest memory is the lights around her, shining through the sea fog, attached to the tugs and rescue vessels and a floating crane. By the time we saw her, it was too late for those little ships to be reaching out to survivors. Now, I would know that this meant that the response had moved from rescue to recovery. But you don't know the official Cabinet Office lexicon for emergency response when you are at primary school.

As we inched towards the wreck, our own cross-Channel ferry slowed down significantly. My dad asked the crew about that later; they said they did it every time they passed so as not to create too much of a wake and further disturb what had been, for a time, a mass grave.

I did not stand silently for long. I had too much to ask. Mainly I wanted to know how people got out. My parents recall me becoming more and more agitated as I queried over and over again that for the people inside, as the boat rolled over, the stairs would be in the wrong place. 'How would they know which way was up?' I asked. It was years before I read testimony from survivors that gave the answer: they didn't and as a result they were horribly discombobulated. As I watched, I knew that there were people still inside the wreck, I could feel it deep inside me. How would they get them out?

But the disaster that was to shape me most profoundly was one which occurred far closer to home. Two years later, on the early evening of Saturday 15 April 1989, I was watching TV with my dad,

who was taking a break from his never-ending task of
making our old wreck of a house habitable. Setting
down his cup of milky tea, he switched the television
on and the coverage had begun reporting on 'an accident' at the FA Cup semi-final between Liverpool
and Nottingham Forest at the Hillsborough Football
Ground in Sheffield. Several of my school classmates
were at the game, as well as colleagues, friends and
pupils of my parents. I remember the room going very
quiet and watching my dad's hands gripping the sides
of the mug, waiting for him to speak. He was a wood-
work teacher and they are carpenter's hands, gnarled
and scarred. One hand is missing a finger from a fight
with a band saw.

My dad called my mum down from a ladder (she
will have been painting something or insulating between
floorboards) to watch with us. They communed in a
series of breathless exchanges. 'This doesn't look like a
pitch invasion' and then several 'bloody hells'.
Eventually one of them said, 'They're using the hoardings . . .?' The fans had broken advertising hoardings
off the stand and were using them to stretcher the
injured. My parents asked each other over and over
again where the ambulances were.

The fatal stadium crush occurred in the central
pens of the Leppings Lane terrace, which was later
found to have no current safety certificate. Ninety-
four people died that day, asphyxiated by the press
of people squashed against the fences after the police
opened a gate. The youngest, Jon-Paul Gilhooley,
was ten years old – the same age as me. A few days

later, fourteen-year-old Lee Nicol died of his injuries and in March 1993, artificial feeding and hydration was removed from twenty-two-year-old Anthony Bland, who had spent four years in a persistent vegetative state. In July 2021, following the death of Andrew Devine, a severely injured survivor, the death toll was amended again. His death, thirty-two years later, brought the final death toll to ninety-seven.

Twenty-three years after Hillsborough, an independent review panel concluded that forty-one of those fans might have been saved if proper medical aid could have been administered. A number of other survivors received devastating injuries that left them requiring lifelong medical assistance and hundreds more suffered physical and mental effects of the disaster. It wrought a terrible toll on my home city.

On the Monday morning after the disaster, at school, normal business – a comprehension test, times tables – was briefly suspended. Our teacher asked us to talk about what we were feeling. She was awkward. I could already read when an adult was struggling. She didn't have the words for us.

Those of us who hadn't been at the game, mainly the girls, were chatty and keen to share their confusion. How had this happened? What was it like? I remember feeling at a disadvantage for not having been there and for only seeing it on television. Later I would come to know this as the hierarchy of disaster grief. The ripples reach far and wide but those in the outer circles have much less claim to feel the effects.

The boy sitting next to me was kneading his eye sockets with his fists. He had been at the stadium with his brothers and his dad. 'I'm just really angry,' he whispered, his face covered. In Birkenhead, in 1989, boys didn't cry. I noticed another boy stayed completely silent. He was a rare Nottingham Forest supporter in a class of almost exclusively Red or Blue and he and his family had been at the other end of the ground, watching the event unfold. All he had been able to do was watch.

The boys in my class played 'Hillsborough' for weeks after the disaster. They would pile on top of each other on the playing field and then carry each other away, one boy to the arms and one boy to the legs. We girls rolled our eyes in mock horror at their silliness.

In other parts of the country, a story was spreading that was to become the official version of events, of drunken and ticketless fans breaking down a gate. From the outset, certain members of the police and club management had promulgated a particular narrative and as early as 3.40 p.m. on the day of the disaster, BBC radio coverage stated that there were 'unconfirmed reports that a door was broken down'. On 19 April, *The Sun* newspaper published an article under the headline 'The Truth' on their front page. Liverpool football fans were accused of pickpocketing the dead, urinating on injured and dying fans and stopping responders from giving first aid. Other national and international newspapers picked up on this position, framing the tragedy as the ultimate low point in British football hooliganism.[4] These accusations about the behaviour of fans were later completely disproved.[5]

My dad brought home a copy of *The Sun* to show my mum. 'Get it out!' was all she said. It was the last time that paper would ever be in our house. About a week after the match, my dad and I were visiting my grandparents in Wavertree, Liverpool, and outside a number of newsagents, people chanted as they burned copies of *The Sun* in braziers. Every time we passed one, my dad slowed and hooted his horn in support. The smell of burning paper always takes me back to that same sky full of smoke, Scouse anger and little bits of black char.

Those months after Hillsborough made me understand that terrible things can happen but also that the people in charge – the state and its agencies – make terrible mistakes. And when they do, often it is the communities that have already been failed who are blamed. Much later, an American colleague would remark on how 'lucky' I was to have made this realisation so early on in my life. It stood me in very good stead later on, when I saw it over and over again. Aged only ten, I also absorbed the pain and anger of my parents. Both of them were fiercely protective of the young lads in their care from the deprived estates of Walton and West Derby, whose worlds had been turned upside down. I remember my dad shouting at the television screen, 'Somebody needs to sort this.' I took that as a direction.

Later in my life, I would come to know that disasters like this force wider change. This is known as the

'Tombstone Imperative'. When safety failings result in a large enough death toll (tombstones) that some form of action becomes essential, the state will acquiesce to a series of legislative changes. Then, once that is done, responders and politicians can set about shifting the tragedy into archive and historical narrative.[6]

Hillsborough also taught me about the longer-term ripples of disaster. The tragedy stayed close to home throughout my teens, as several friends battled to process their demons. I witnessed the wear of years of legal battles, health complications and trauma. My friend's dad had survived the crush, lifting his nephew over his head to safety, but had been left severely injured. He also suffered terribly with bouts of anger, flashbacks and insomnia. As teenage girls, we thought he was grumpy and protective but I know now that he was traumatised and suffering from one of the most crippling effects of surviving disaster: the grieving for the life that went before. Of course, that is not just true of disaster but of many other types of bereavement and injury and loss. You wake up with a set of hopes and expectations but then, later that same day, something big and terrible happens and bang, nothing is ever the same again. As a survivor of disaster, even if you are not physically injured you might lose your sense of safety, your trust in the authorities and you may encounter a number of mental health challenges that can cripple you. You are not the person you were before. The man your family loved on 14 April 1989 or 10 September 2001 or 13 June 2017 is still here physically but some of who he was before is lost and the rest of the family mourn for that part of him. In my experience, and in my generation, it is often the dads who seem to be particularly badly affected by this. They were expected to be able to keep their tribe safe from harm and the realisation that they can't hits them very hard.

By the time I was a teenager, I had become obsessed by disaster and wider social causes. The disaster work I do now is multi-disciplinary, drawing on law, forensic science, politics and social justice and activism, and I can trace much of these specialisms back to these years. I was an unusual, 'determined' teenager. In a time of New Kids on the Block and Take That, *Sabrina the Teenage Witch* and Nickelodeon, it was hard to find acceptance for my fledgling disaster activism and a variety of additional social causes. I would check out books on dictators, the Second World War, nuclear power and famine from the library. I wrote to government ministers, celebrities, the royal family, *Private Eye* and Mother Teresa. This interest in all of the worst things society does prepared me well for the breadth of disaster management later on; doctors study medicine and lawyers, the law, but disaster planning and management conferences can leap from lessons in human geography to palliative care, traffic management to the disposal of radioactive waste. There might be a workshop on aviation crew resource management or an evening lecture from a survivor of Chernobyl.

I also spent as much of my summer holidays as I could with my aunty and uncle, a husband and wife duo who both happened to be coroners in different northern towns. Coroners are senior and independent judges who investigate 'sudden, violent or unnatural death' in England and Wales but also use this recurring set of tragic case studies to try to prevent future harms to society.[7] They use a form of prospective foresight for future harms and regularly submit 'Prevention of Future Death' reports. Whenever 'work experience week' came around I signed up, enthusiastically, to hang out with Uncle Mike and Aunty Cal and their colleagues. Later in my career, I would be working hand-in-hand with coroners on disaster recovery; in fact, I am in contact with them most days. Many would become close friends and fierce allies.

Time with coroners, and also on placements with Liverpudlian barristers and solicitors, gave me an intense respect for our legal system and in 1997, I was awarded a place on a 'widening participation' scheme to study law at the University of Bristol, designed to encourage more students from lower income backgrounds into the university. If I had 'the law', maybe I could challenge the system from within, I thought. I was excited to get a place but I never felt like I fitted in at Bristol. Every rite and ritual was unfamiliar: hall dinners, formal dress, food fights and slang. There were students who were close friends of princes and destined to be future politicians. Some had limitless credit cards and were sent hampers from Harrods and Fortnum and Mason by their families on a Saturday.

Meanwhile, the families and survivors in Liverpool were still trying every possible avenue of every branch of the legal system: private prosecutions, reviews, re-openings of inquests, public inquiries, judicial reviews. There had been divorces, suicides and fragmentation of the support groups. In my summer holidays, I interned at the Centre for Crime and Social Justice in Lancashire for Phil Scraton, the criminologist who was growing in prominence as a leading campaigner fighting for justice after Hillsborough. I would make myself scarce in the library when the retired South Yorkshire police officers who turned up at Phil's office on the Ormskirk campus came for a cup of tea and a chance to unburden. These were officers who had felt pressure to redact and alter their version of events and had carried the weight of the truth for more than a decade.[8]

Hillsborough was a key topic in the legal world at the time and became the subject of much debate in my classes, though I was shocked to discover that most of my fellow students in Bristol believed the fans had orchestrated their own demise. I read judgements in the law reports that were painfully damning of the fans' behaviour and even my tutor used to mimic the Harry Enfield 'Scousers' sketches when he read out the quotes, the room descending into mocking 'calm downs'. One afternoon, while we waited to file into the lecture theatre, the corridor started to fill up. 'Hey!' shouted an acquaintance. 'Don't get too close to Lucy – we all know how people from Liverpool behave in crowds.'

As I was the butt of many jokes in my halls of residence about being a combative Scouser, I decided to partially embrace the stereotype. I started replacing the copies of the *Daily Telegraph* and *The Times* in the junior common room with the *Liverpool Echo*. And I took a job as a security guard at the union to supplement my student loan. I earned £80 a night as one of four female guards on the team. I joined the combat karate club as the other guards were members. Though I had early onset arthritis and severe dyspraxia, which didn't help make me a natural and the teacher suggested I might like to be in charge of refreshments.

One night at the end of an indie rock gig, a crush built up outside one of the exits. The union had a spiral staircase that ran right through the middle of the building. This staircase had always made me uneasy; we had headed off a number of near-misses here, including lifting people off the banister when they had been so drunk they thought they could fly. Now, the surge of concert goers had pushed a young lad who fell over the banister and down through the middle of several floors before landing at my feet. By that time in my life I had already seen a number of people punched in the face and there is a distinctive noise when a fist meets facial bones. The sound of this boy landing in front of me was like that magnified by a thousand.

Every limb appeared to be at the wrong angle, like a marionette puppet, and blood was already pouring from his face. His eye appeared to be distorted in its socket and I could see urine spreading from underneath him. He made no sounds, for which I am eternally grateful, and did not regain consciousness the whole time I was with him. The paramedics told us later that the alcohol he had consumed would have worked to numb the pain. I covered him in a coat and yelled at people not to move him in case we broke his neck. I had done a first aid course a couple of years earlier but if I'm honest, I was thinking more of the hundreds of episodes of the TV hospital drama *Casualty* I'd watched through my teenage years. As he was joined by his friends, some of them were so bladdered that they tried to haul him up by his broken arms. Eventually we clumsily attempted the recovery position and I sat next to him as his blood and piss soaked my trousers as well as his. We were all fairly certain he was dead and the girl from St John Ambulance started being sick in a bin. There was some confusion between the senior staff members on duty, both assuming the other had called 999 and the ambulance seemed to take an age. Once he had been taken away to hospital, we discharged the rest of the punters out into the night air, on auto-pilot.

That night, I wrote my first post-incident report. I handed it in to the union managers the next day. I found it recently and it is the best one I have ever written – it was without guile or politics and complete with a set of carefully constructed recommendations. The university management emphasised that the incident was completely unforeseeable. The report in the student newspaper drew attention to how drunk the student was and later I read articles that mocked him for being a student of our neighbouring former polytechnic, the University of the West of England, rather than Bristol and for liking indie rock. It all felt horribly familiar.

For me, it was a vital lesson in being on the other side of the disaster. Suddenly, crushingly, I had a tiny insight into what it might be like to be a police constable at South Yorkshire Police. I had a brief taste of being one of the corporate team who is wearing the t-shirt of the institution that has caused harm but ultimately is terribly conflicted. I didn't want the injured chap mocked. I didn't want the university's lawyers to try to dismiss his compensation claim, due to his insobriety. But I was on the team whose fault it was, so you suck it up.

I learned a lot about blame and post-disaster corporate response that night. The young man survived, albeit with many broken bones but fortunately no paralysis. The staircase is still there.

2

Bad Stars

The word 'disaster' is formed from the Latin *dis* and *astro*, meaning bad stars. It refers to an ancient belief that when the stars are in a bad position, unfortunate events are going to occur. A misaligning of the astronomical bodies sends the world off kilter. On an individual level, a disaster might be losing our job, our relationship or just our keys. But an official disaster – a 'major incident' as English planners are now told to call it – is something at quite a different scale.[9] Something that most of us don't expect or anticipate. We don't think about disasters until they are on the news, after they happen.

But I cannot imagine living my life like that. I have always found myself analysing what might happen and why. Since I was a child, I have always tried to be the first to know about the perils all around and ahead of us. When we were learning about the Great War, I wanted to linger on the pandemic of 1918, straight after it. When we learned about Florence Nightingale, I wanted to know more about the Crimean War, less about the lamp. I was fascinated by stories of 'Typhoid

Mary' – the ultimate super spreader – and the way that she spread her pestilence around hundreds of households in New York. The second that I hear about a new potential disaster risk I start weighing up its impact. The immediate consequences and effects on those around its epicentre.

During my student years, I began to find others who thought the same way. In their case, though, it wasn't an innate fascination that drew them to disaster. On the contrary, this was a club nobody wanted to be in. They were the survivors and families of the many mass fatality incidents that had punctuated the eighties and nineties in the UK and they had formed themselves into a support and advocacy group, Disaster Action.

I found them without knowing to look for them. In 1999, Dr Anne Eyre was a young academic who had dedicated the first decade of her working life to improving the care of people after disasters. As a 21-year-old PhD student, she had been trapped in the Leppings Lane crush at Hillsborough. Anne was the first ever person that I sent an email to, using the first ever email account that I was given. Gingerly putting my brand new knowledge of search engines to use, I had found her name and email address at the top of an article about survivors' proactive responses to disaster. I asked her if there were ways I could help with her work and Anne generously and effusively replied with an invitation to a conference. I borrowed the train fare from my mum and dad and headed off to my first encounter with this group that would fundamentally shape the way I thought about disaster and change me forever.

Seeing a procession of survivors and relatives in one space was a shocking and inescapable visual representation of the continuum of disasters and the conditions that cause them. Suddenly my Hillsborough rage was layered with other injustices. The 1980s and 1990s had been a particularly brutal time in British disaster experience; lives totalling thousands had been lost in a series of socio-technical failings. Trains and planes, stadiums, parties on a boat, oil rigs, ferries. All of these disasters had been preventable. One air crash after another. One rail crash after another; almost identical sets of incubating circum-stances. There was solace for these people in Disaster Action, as well as strength in numbers. Collective voices campaigning on the same issues can shout louder.[10]

Disaster Action campaigned for lessons to be learned and better support for families. As time went on, they danced a delicate ballet of having seats at many government tables while staying fiercely independent and necessarily critical. I was in awe of their diplomacy and their gentle question-ing. Their strength and their patience as they explained to yet another hatchling civil servant about the key principles of caring for people caught up in a major incident was inspiring. Ministers slowly started to listen as sisters and fathers, husbands and sons gave keynote speeches to trade unions, local authorities, police forces and airlines.

The crux of their message: that if more thought was given, at the early stages, to those affected by disaster, the authorities could avoid piling up misery on the already traumatised.

In contrast to my struggle to find my place at Bristol, I was always made welcome at these events. I was often the youngest there. I would be warmly greeted with a peck on the cheek by the spritely Italian Vincenzo Dallaglio. He had lost his daughter when the *Marchioness* was dragged beneath the Thames. She was a talented ballerina. Vincenzo was also the father of English rugby star Lawrence Dallaglio. I never plucked up the courage to tell Vincenzo that for most of the 1990s I had been hoping to marry his son.

This was also where I met Maureen Kavanagh for the first time. Peter, her son, had been a twenty-nine-year-old environmental lawyer who was killed in the Southall train crash in 1997. Moments before the driver went through a red signal and crashed into a freight train, Peter had called his mum to tell her he loved her 'big as the world' and that he would see her later.

In the months and years that followed, somehow Maureen found the strength, over and over again, to pull on her coat and head to police training events and to safety conferences. In the initial aftermath, she had listened to the police refer to her beloved, handsome boy as 'body number seven'. Later, another officer had told her that Peter was sleeping when he died in a crude attempt to soothe her. She knew that to be untrue because he had been speaking to her just seconds before. This well-intentioned lie made her question anything that the police and the coroner told her.

She campaigned for better training for coroners, more rights for families and better care of the bereaved. Maureen became a powerhouse for change in disaster prevention, too. She was instrumental in reforming corporate manslaughter legislation. She didn't want anyone else to go through her pain. I remember in one of our earliest interactions I marvelled to her at how she managed to fit everything in – all the campaigning and the fighting. For a second her face became unbearably sad and still. 'I do it at night,' she said quietly. 'I don't sleep any more you see.' She was often asked where her strength came from and she would answer that the worst thing that could have happened to her had happened and that gave her a kind of power.

So often it was the mums and sisters who would continue the fight for justice. Later, this would remind me of the groups of campaigning *madres* in Central American countries like Guatemala, where thousands of people have been 'disappeared' since the 1960s. So whenever I think of Disaster Action, I think of them as *madres*, though of course there were fathers and brothers and sons too, and indeed the founder of Disaster Action was a father, Maurice de Rohan, who had lost his children in the *Herald of Free Enterprise* disaster. Collectively, the members of Disaster Action were a forceful reminder that the deceased in disasters are not just bodies or sets of remains. They are as important and present in death as they had been in life.

By 1998 I had also fallen in love. In my second year of university, I moved into a house share, via a friend's friend, and there was Tom. While I was cheerful and bouncy, he was a painfully shy aeronautical engineering student intensely contemplating the meaning of life, fuelled by a love of Radiohead and Pink Floyd's *Dark Side of the Moon* album. I bounced into his life, the yin to his yang, his polar opposite. All he wanted to do was fly commercial airliners but struggled on with a degree he clearly hated. If that was the dream, why not pursue it? I urged, as only a new girlfriend flooded with oxytocin can.

He was incredibly able technically but struggled to overcome his shyness in interviews and the group tasks so prized by airline recruitment managers. I coached him relentlessly and sat in airport coffee shops when I should have been in land law lectures while he struggled through group exercises in which he and six others had to pretend to build a raft on a desert island. I spent my nights researching how you became a commercial pilot and learned that you were much more employable when you already had the necessary licences and ratings. I also discovered that learning to fly and building up hours in the United States is common practice for trainee UK pilots because the fuel is cheaper and the weather more clement. Together we set about borrowing enough from family and friends and banks to head to America.

I spent my holidays from university and my student loan visiting Tom at a flight school in Florida. Huffman Aviation was a school with a fleet of twelve small planes in the city of Venice. The small airfield was close to the beach and surrounded by malls, an Irish bar, hotels, churches and an all-you-can-eat Chinese buffet. Tom spent months flying a Diamond DA20 Katana from Venice to Sarasota. I would sit on the beach, famous for its fossilised shark teeth, squinting up at what I hoped was his plane. The sky would buzz with little single engine crafts, all doing the same thing.

After graduating with my law degree, I was keen to get started on the next step of saving the universe but not entirely sure how to go about it. My dad was a friend of the scriptwriter Jimmy McGovern – they had taught together when Jimmy had been an English teacher in West Derby – and Jimmy was now well known for his work on Hillsborough. He suggested I apply for a job as a researcher for renowned TV producer Katy Jones. She was known for her exposition of social injustices and had worked on the investigative documentary series *World in Action*. She took me on to work on the production of *Sunday*, about the events of Bloody Sunday in Northern Ireland in 1972. We were based in frenetic production offices co-habited by teams from both Channel 4 and Granada Television in a heady melee of pop groups and soap stars. I was the only young woman working in the dream job of television, it seemed, who was saving up to do something else. I lived at home, spending my spare cash on care parcels for Tom and attending disaster conferences.

At the start of the new millennium, I found a university offering a master's degree in disaster management and took out another student loan. The course, still offered today, at the University of Leicester was designed for busy professionals already working in risk management, for charities and in the security services. My fellow students on modules about properly understanding and applying disaster case studies, how to communicate terrible risks and why companies fail, worked for organisations from the United Nations and Lloyds Bank to Mars and Nike.

Meanwhile, as Tom was earning his qualifications at Huffman, a group of young men wrote to the administrator of his flight school enquiring about the chance of an intensive programme to get them up to commercial flight standards, too. Their applications were successful. Later, these men – Mohamed Atta, Ziad Jarrah and Marwan al-Shehhi – also learned to fly at Huffman Aviation. They parked on the same forecourt as we had and flew the same planes on the same routes. They were issued their pilot licences in December 2000.

Nine months later they and sixteen others used boxcutters and brute strength to force their way into the cockpits of four jets and flew them directly at sites of totemic importance across America. That afternoon, 11 September 2001, I was at home in Birkenhead having a day or two's respite from the frenetic activity of working on TV programmes while studying for my master's. Twelve years after Hillsborough, I once again watched the footage of an unfolding disaster sat next to my dad. This time it was on an apocalyptic scale. We watched live as fire tore through the trading floors of the World Trade Center and people jumped from windows 400 metres up. Normal broadcasting was suspended, including all of the children's TV. My dad set off down our street to alert all neighbours with young children not to turn their television sets on.

One hundred and two minutes after the two planes had crashed into the World Trade Center, both towers collapsed. A total of 2,977 people were killed in New York City, Washington, DC and outside of Shanksville, Pennsylvania; 2,753 of them at the World Trade Center site. The youngest was two, the oldest eighty five.

Earlier that year, just six months before the attacks, I had attended a conference on planning for the worst. A senior civil servant told the audience it was important to be realistic – 'Let's have no more planning for planes crashing into buildings. Keep your plans REAL,' he said with a flourish. Three years later, the commission report into the circumstances of the attacks would describe this belief as 'The Failure of Imagination'.[11]

This was the catalyst for me. It was time to move away from the world of television and plant my professional feet where they really belonged. This almost inevitably led me to Kenyon International

Emergency Services. Kenyon is the oldest of a very small number of private companies who are hired by organisations and governments when the worst happens. They offer a beginning-to-end disaster management service for the right price, in the direst of circumstances. Scene management, temporary mortuaries, repatriation, family liaison, burial and cremation arrangements. The company had begun as a large funeral directing firm in London and had been operating for almost a century, starting out with rail crashes and even an airship disaster. Taking a job with them was a way to get as close as possible to the epicentre of a disaster. On the quieter days, you might run exercises or re-review a plan but you lived your life ready to respond to the real thing, and this happened almost weekly. Corporate jets, the aftermath of hurricanes, an overturned ferry ... There's plenty that can go wrong if you're willing to think about it.

The forensic aftermath of the 9/11 attacks pushed disaster response teams to new frontiers of evidence gathering and preservation. The teams in America were so stretched that they needed support and Kenyon was employed by the Office of Chief Medical Examiner (OCME) New York City to assist with the scene management, personal effects, body storage and the mortuary. This work would become the biggest disaster forensics deployment in history.

The two UK Kenyon managers interviewed me through a fug of cigarette smoke and gave me a £200 budget to buy a dark suit for funerals and cargo trousers with lots of pockets for the disaster scene. I was in. Immediately I was tasked with sourcing British mortuary and funeral personnel who could be sent over to work at the scene, Ground Zero, and in the facilities storing the personal effects and human remains. I was given a list of names and numbers and got to work assembling a team.[12]

Everything about 9/11 added complications and challenges. The death toll, the politics and the scene itself. A thick powder of over thirty-one cancer-causing chemicals had coated the remains and the personal effects and still hung heavy in the air. From the earliest days of the aftermath of 9/11, we, alongside many other responders, survivors and local Manhattan residents, asked for help with this dust. I tentatively lobbied for better breathing apparatus and equipment for our team to no avail, while tiny particles of contamination burrowed into Ground Zero responders' lungs. Soon there were reports of a 'Ground Zero cough' and later, testing would show the multiple carcinogens that were present in that dust, including asbestos, mercury, chromium and zinc.[13] Nearly a decade later, 'September 11th Respiratory Disease' was recognised as a genuine health effect of exposure to that dust and a $657.5 million fund was created to compensate clean-up workers at the scene. I learned a lot then about the haste of disaster response and how we pay for that haste for many years. Just a slight pause to test the dust, to risk assess and to procure better equipment would have made a profound difference.

When the towers collapsed, they also created new levels of complexity for the forensic response. In the medical examiner's office, the earliest post-mortem numbers were given to those who died from head injuries from falling masonry or when another person fell on to them from above. They were dragged off the streets and into the care of the medical examiner as soon as possible. The first recorded death, or 'victim 0001', was Father Mychal Judge, the chaplain to the New York City fire department, who had been one of the first to the scene to offer his prayers and was hit from falling debris in the North Tower. His body was recovered before the towers went down and his earlier prayers were captured on film by a French TV crew and a number of press photographs. But minutes later, when the towers collapsed, they took with them, and buried, so many of those who might have survived. The heat, pressure and, later, water changed the nature of what would be recovered from their bodies. For many of the deceased, what was left was often only fragments, or nothing at all. The medical examiner readied his team for the bodies but in fact the site was so hard to excavate that few came.

The medical examiner made an early promise to families to identify as much of their loved one as scientifically as possible and then to make arrangements to inter any unidentifiable remains in a mausoleum at the site some time in the future. They pledged that as science adapted and evolved, they would always evaluate this decision. While the commitment to leave no stone unturned in identifying the dead was laudable, understandable and humane, it sent a shiver of disquiet through some of us in the disaster response community. Binding themselves to a policy that lay at the edge of what was scientifically possible with no exit strategy felt like the kind of early decision that can keep the wounds of the bereaved open indefinitely.

To keep that promise, the forensic scientists were desperate to slow the deterioration of the tiny fragments. I was involved in the procurement and delivery of hundreds of cookie trays for them to lay out flesh and bone. Sometimes the human tissue resembled delicate flakes of filo pastry, sandwiched between concrete and fabric or wrapped in the protective layer of a fire officer's jacket. They also salvaged tiny little balls of paper – the sort of thing you fish out of the washing machine when you have accidentally left a till receipt in your coat pocket. Quite often they *were* till receipts and, in one case, one of these was found in a pair of damaged trousers that could be returned to a grieving mother. She said she found a glimmer of comfort knowing her son had had a coffee and a croissant for breakfast that morning. Occasionally, the knots of paper would be unravelled to reveal notes written by people as they were trapped inside the two towers. One said simply: *84th Floor west office 12 People trapped.* The blood-stained fingerprint on it was later tested for DNA and provided as confirmation to the family that their father, Randy Scott, had been in that place before he died.

The total count for fragments recovered in New York after the attacks on 9/11 is around 22,000 and a regular breakdown of the data is provided by the medical examiner. Many families received multiple sets of remains over a number of years. Al and Ginger Petrocelli's son Mark had been a commodities trader in the World Trade Center. Confirmation that there was a DNA match between his profile and tissue samples found actually came early on in the response[14] but tiny pieces of Mark then continued to be released to his family. By the time of the second anniversary of the attacks, his family had gathered together five times to bury a new set of remains in a Staten Island cemetery. Responders pioneered an approach of opting the families in or out of this process but it was far from perfect.

In spite of all this painstaking work, however, there has still been no physical connection made between a body part and a person's name on a list in 40 per cent of cases of all those who died in New York on 9/11. So four in ten mothers, fathers, brothers, sisters, partners, wives, husbands and children have never had any human remains returned but instead rely on personal effects, voicemail messages, anecdotal stories of passing in stairwells and financial and phone records that suggest or show they were there. Their mourning had to take place often in an absence of certainty and without a body to bury.

The recovery of identity at the World Trade Center in New York has been one of the biggest and most enduring ever attempted. The Office of Chief Medical Examiner spent billions on a futuristic laboratory that would fulfil their promises to families. The facility shares a wall with the 9/11 museum and there is a room in it accessible only to bereaved families, where they can sit close to the remains.

The labs are shiny and futuristic and, two decades later, the unending quest to identify remains feels a bit like how the quest to travel to space might feel in a NASA facility. For some families, this has been a comfort; to others, the opposite. It would have offended something deep within us to have simply lowered those bodies into a mass grave or never to have troubled to find them in the first place. But perhaps it is also true that the human spirit needs in the end to draw a line, to find a way to let the bones and the bodies rest.

By the summer of 2002, our workload continued to expand in New York and around the world. 9/11 may have been the biggest but it was not the only disaster we were working on. Planes crashed and boats sank elsewhere, while the world mostly watched four sites in the USA. A disaster response that had 'gone quiet' would need my attention again: suddenly a new shipment of personal effects or more access to a scene would require a shift of focus. We would find ourselves revisiting a tragedy from a year before, preparing families for new pain. One day I would be the gopher and the odd job lady – holding equipment during a post-mortem, bagging up personal effects, labelling samples for DNA testing and ordering new supplies. The next day I might be charged out at $3,500 US dollars a day to a client who needed a mortuary plan with a full risk assessment. (I didn't see the fee.) There were also days where I would give the tiny kitchen a good clean or wait for the repair man to fix our office TV.

After a series of tests of my readiness, such as heading up a personal effects team in the warehouse and taking my first activation call from a global airline following a crash, I was finally put in charge of the first deployment that I would lead on. I was alone in the office when the call came in to say that a helicopter belonging to one of our clients had downed in the North Sea off the Norfolk coast. A mixture of nerves and excitement ran through me as I realised my managers were both involved in work on 9/11 so I was going to have to handle this response alone. Before I had a chance to protest, I was told to go and collect a hire car and head down there. I hung up the phone and thought through my options. Most pressingly, I had to get to Norfolk.

At the Kenyon interview, we had never discussed whether I could drive and it wasn't on the application form; they just assumed I could. By this time, my childhood clumsiness had been formally diagnosed as dyspraxia and meant I had never got my licence. So I persuaded a new friend and colleague, Alan, to take us down there. Alan is first and foremost a funeral director, one of society's most necessary and undervalued roles, there to usher families through what may be one of the most difficult weeks of their entire lives. He has taught me the value of dressing smartly, smiling warmly and leading the family through. He and I had bonded over the previous weeks while drawing up a database for the latest consignment of personal effects from an air crash in Italy. I had found him to be compassionate and generous but I also liked him because he looked like a naughty Father Christmas and shared my filthy sense of humour and love of food.

By the time we arrived at the police station, it was already early evening and starting to get dark. Like a honeymooning couple in a ghost story, Alan and I were shown to a creepy wooden outbuilding with a grimy chest freezer pushed against one wall. The officer watched us uneasily as the freezer lid was heaved open.

'We didn't know what to do with them,' the officer said defensively, as we peered in. Here were coats, rucksacks, wellington boots and chequebooks, soaked with blood, human tissue and seawater, all frozen into grotesque ice lollies. We knew that as they melted, they would leak copious amounts of bloody brine. There is a myth around forensics that freezing is used as a preservation technique but generally for both bodies and personal effects it can cause further damage (it is used for DNA swabs, fluid samples and the long-term storage of evidence for the courts).

The helicopter passengers were employees of an oil company, travelling between a gas production platform and a drilling rig and then on to Norwich airport. Men on the nearby rigs had heard an explosion and then watched in horror as the helicopter plummeted into the sea. They were trained to record the location of a crash site and so they pointed, arms outstretched, at the area of the choppy North Sea as the helicopter sank, leaving behind rainbow slicks of fuel. The investigation report said they stayed pointing like that until help arrived and I imagined their arms throbbing and cramping with the effort.

Debris and four deceased were recovered immediately. There was hopeful talk of survivors, which faded to acceptance that all eleven men on board had died. The search for their bodies went on for days. The crash had been caused by a manufacturing anomaly in the rotor blade, exacerbated by a previous lightning strike, which had further weakened the fault. The force of the loss of the blade had been hugely disruptive and caused severe fragmentation of some of the deceased. Only ten bodies have ever been found. There may be one collective death toll in a disaster but the actual recovery of each of the deceased can take many weeks, months or never happen at all. Every new day can turn up another grim discovery. And a hierarchy can emerge where those families who have a body are considered 'lucky' compared to those who don't.

We were hired by the commercial owners of the helicopter and the oil company to manage the aftermath, in particular to sort out the items belonging to the dead men. For the police, these items are evidence and exhibits but they are also precious objects that we in disaster response call 'personal effects' and their treatment forms a large part of my job. In this case, I had to slowly thaw out and inventory each item, including anything within pockets or bags. As these items warmed, the full olfactory impact of sea water, mildew, blood and shit hit me. I thought a lot about the shit and prayed that it had happened as the last act of an already brain-dead body. I didn't want them to have felt any fear.

The Norfolk deployment was the first of many times that I would check into a cheap B&B with my own suitcase as well as items of still-thawing luggage of several dead men. I placed the items in the bath. I slept badly, worrying about how I would get it all safely outside if the fire alarm went off. The next morning, Alan and I drove these items to our processing warehouse, a bleak cavern surrounded by other industrial units and a car dealership in Bracknell. It was opposite a greasy spoon café and my new co-workers would start most days with a Gut Buster breakfast, which I could never quite find the stomach for.

I was in charge of the keys to the warehouse but I hated arriving there first, scrabbling in the dark alone for the switches to the fluorescent lighting. The warehouse was filled with trestles, on which sat boxes and boxes of flip flops and sandals. A tray of watches. We used to describe things as 'silver' or 'Gucci' but experience has again taught us not to assume, so now we write, 'silver-like/grey metal' and 'a label with the word Gucci on it'. Across the back of the cavernous space was a washing line drying pieces of paper: letters, shopping lists, bank notes, religious texts.

After a brief spell in a rented room with a landlady and her cats, Tom and I had taken the step of renting a flat in a block around the corner from the main Kenyon offices in Harrow. Our view was a busy street corner and a set of traffic lights, where local boy-racers gathered on a Friday and Saturday. The very first time that Tom had called to pick me up from work, wearing his new airline uniform, one of my colleagues had joked that we had several of those uniforms drying in the personal effects warehouse from a crash in Germany. From then on, I caught the bus home.

It took months to sort through all the items from the helicopter crash and in that time it felt as though an invisible gauze was slowly forming between me and the rest of the world. I would stand at the doorway of the warehouse wondering at the people walking by unaware. I have worked in all areas of disaster response – including supporting grieving families, in the mortuary and repatriating remains from overseas – but Alan warned me that the 'hardest' work of all was returning personal effects. I think he may have been right. Unpacking the personal rucksacks belonging to these men felt like the most grotesque invasion of privacy.

All those who had died were men and their property represented some sort of generalisation of their age and their gender: branded underpants, wash bags with Gillette razor blades and shaving foam. At home in the evenings, exhausted, I would stare for a long time at Tom's identical wash bag in our bathroom.

★   ★   ★

A centre piece in the Kenyon offices was shelf after shelf, an entire wall, of blue box files crammed with the paper notes from each deployment, stretching back to 1906. It towered over us; to reach the top shelf required a ladder. This wall of files felt like a physical representation of the way that disasters slam at us one after the other. Sometimes there would be ten or twelve 'mass fatality events' in a year, perhaps two in the same month after several weeks of quiet. Some on our shores, others involving our citizens or a UK client overseas.

These files could rarely be closed, consigned to archive; there would often be new items to add to the box decades later – a newspaper clipping or a letter from a legal team. Over the years, papers had been misfiled, so on our quieter days I reorganised them. I ordered a new label maker and sat on the floor, on the old stained carpet, with the boxes and their contents all around me. Polaroids of the dead from fifty different incidents spilled out of post-mortem files. Mortuary plans written in engineer's blue ink. Handwritten lists of the dead. I was fascinated by those boxes. They were a demonstration of something also signified by the Disaster Action families: the repeated *dis* and *astro* – the badly aligned stars, over and over again. All connected by hidden silvery threads, rarely seen by the rest of society. I laid my hands on each one.

I was overwhelmed by how many there are and how many there will always be. No human action can ever stop sudden, unexpected tragedy completely. But these boxes also reinforced in me something else. The papers in the boxes were not about the disaster itself but records of the actions of those who had gone to assist. As long as there were disasters, there would also be people heading out to help.

3

In Green and Pleasant Lands

I was tasked with building the mortuary before the soldiers in Iraq were dead. A shopping list was faxed to us and I watched as it was slowly spat out of the machine:

500 x body bags
750 x coffins
750 x coffin liners
750 x flags
250 x body bags for chemically contaminated deceased

This was just the initial list. We were told to prepare for several thousand deceased and for the possibility they might have been contaminated by chemical and biological agents. If Saddam used the weapons supposedly at his disposal the consequences were almost unthinkable.

In autumn of 2002, I was working for Kenyon when the Ministry of Defence approached us to support the repatriation of any personnel killed during the invasion of Iraq. My bosses told me I was being promoted to planning and operations lead. The logistics of making sure a potential mortuary had everything it needed would be my responsibility. I had to turn that fax into a reality. I got started on my macabre treasure hunt, sourcing flags and coffins and body bags, while our prime minister, Tony Blair, went back and forth to the United Nations.

As my work at Kenyon started to become all-consuming, work and home became more and more separate. The gauze had thickened, creating two distinct 'swim lanes'. I became inarticulate when trying to explain my working day to my family and friends, and I was conscious of drifting from Tom. War was not guaranteed and the fact that a mortuary was being built was highly sensitive, so I did not speak about it. It was good planning to build it in advance but an anathema while the 'Stop the War' marches were still underway. It suggested a done deal.

But as the war began to look increasingly likely, I knew that my small team and I would be away for weeks at a time. Before I left, Tom and I attempted a series of 'date nights', which were all highly unsuccessful. I was trying to use the very brief calm before the storm to grab some time together but I felt unable to tell Tom what was preoccupying me. On a visit to the cinema, I spent the end of the film in the loo taking a call about the difference between 'theatre' coffins that would be used in the war zone and 'coffins for best' that would be paraded out of the Hercules plane and in front of royalty. I turned down invites to birthday parties and a weekend back home with Tom's family. When his grandfather died, I took more phone calls from the funeral director's car, parked next to the freshly dug grave. Like most people, Tom assumed that war was a military matter, so couldn't fully understand my involvement or the intimacy I would have with its dead.

Looking back, I never had a conversation with him about why this work was so important to me and how, when working with the deceased and the grieving, we often had only one chance to get this right.

Tom took these abandonments well, on reflection, and he too was working long hours on very early and very late shifts with an airline. But they nonetheless created a distance between us and our companionship relied on snatched moments between each other's worlds.

I have never been afraid of the dead, I think of them as my kin. I was taught early on about the beauty of decomposition and the way that we break down into our constituent chemicals and minerals, so dead bodies, in whatever state, have never horrified me, although the stories they tell sometimes do. Some bodies seem hunted or mauled while others are almost untouched by their injuries. They are the action movie cliché; the body that looks like it is sleeping, just a smudge over the eyebrow, the hint of a stomach turning green. But otherwise perfect, even beautiful.

One time, early on in my career, I was first to arrive at a night-time post-mortem and when I saw the man lying on the metal table, I laughed. My colleagues had been pranking me all week, trying to get the new girl to wobble, and I recognised one of them lying there pretending to be dead. I tiptoed up to him to get as close as I could and then whispered 'boo' in his ear. Nothing. When I looked closer I saw he was not in fact my colleague but a near-perfect doppelganger, brought in earlier that night from the incident, quite dead. I have learned many times since that coincidences that seem to belong only in Stephen King stories actually happen in disasters all the time.

I am at home in a disaster mortuary. I feel protected, buffered from the rest of the world, including the bereaved. The smell is linked to a thousand memories. So many texts, from pathology manuals to true-crime thrillers, have tried to describe the scent of decomposing bodies but there really is nothing like it. There are some similar compounds in fresh-cut grass, semen, particular vegetables, animal meat and menstrual blood but nothing replicates the totality of its assault on your nasal passages. It has put me off mushrooms for life. In the mortuary, this entwines with the penetrating perfume of a particular cleaning fluid. More often than not, the same product is used in mortuaries as in schools and hospitals, in countries all around the world. I've found this particular cleaning fluid has a canny, fateful habit of turning up at the wrong moment. In the toilets of a concert venue on an anniversary night out. Mopped in the corridors of the many emergency gynae wards I have visited in the last decade. The products of death and life and loss.

We built the main Iraq war mortuary at RAF Brize Norton, Oxfordshire, a huge base for the nation's air force, in the weeks before the proposed invasion. When a disaster occurs with mass fatalities, local mortuaries will usually not have the space to care for the bodies, so temporary mortuaries are built. Sometimes they are just large marquees, the kind that are supplied for weddings and outdoor summer gatherings; other times they are more elaborate structures made from the fabric and framing that is used for military camps. Existing spaces such as sports halls or military hangars may also be commandeered and repurposed. The least successful approach is to attempt to tack on storage to existing facilities, already loaded with the 'everyday' dead.

Even though this was military action, the deceased would still be under the jurisdiction of a local coroner when they got back here; the local authority always funds the facilities required for sudden or unexpected death and so they employed Kenyon for the repatriation and a mortuary facility. The government advisers had spent some time trying to work out where the mortuary would go and who the coroner would be. They had drawn up a list of 'good' coroners who would be compliant, and 'naughty' coroners who might come up with a rogue verdict, like misadventure due to an illegal war.[15] I was amused to see that my uncle Mike was on the latter. As an airbase, Brize Norton was set up to receive military aircraft and therefore geared towards repatriation and early on edged forward as a favourite. Oxfordshire's council tax payers would take a hit for our national invasion of Iraq.

We built the mortuary in the base's gymnasium. The service men and women had been using this space to work out and play basketball, badminton and football as they got ready for war. There was a notice-board dedicated to the expeditions run by the skiing club. I felt extremely bad about taking this away from them and turning it into a morgue. You can see the basketball net and the court markings in the forensic photographs that were taken of the deceased. Some of the more sadistic fitness instructors made new recruits run around the perimeters of the body storage units.

From then on in my career, when developing mortuary plans, I would advise planners to give considerable thought to the location and the long-term effects of stigma on the place once used. There are many tales of schools and municipal spaces being changed in the eyes of their local community. One of the most infamous is the ice rink in Sarajevo where Torvill and Dean won Olympic gold in 1984 for their ice dancing to the 'Bolero'. After it was used as a mortuary and then burned down in the later fighting, memories of the dead blotted out the rink's past glories. It was rebuilt a decade later so that people could dance there again.

Disaster mortuaries have to be ready for all kinds of remains. Contaminated or diseased; bloated and bariatric, rapidly decomposing after drowning; cremains, the tiny fragments of bone and flesh after a fire. One of the first briefings that the chair of the Mass Fatalities Co-ordinating Group will have asked for is a description of the remains and what this will mean for the process of recovering the fragments and of identification.

I divided the mortuary plan into areas representing key functions. I learned on the job for this, my first, but Kenyon also had a hundred floor plans from years and years of responding. The Oklahoma bombing mortuary. The Piper Alpha oil platform fire mortuary. I studied these like an archaeologist. Mortuaries from nearly a hundred different air disasters around the world. Almost all follow the same formula. There are 'wet' areas for the post-mortem work – a series of tables and taps and enough room for tens of personnel. There are 'dry' areas for administration and examining records. I have spent many hours getting the flow chart of functions right. I learned through mistakes. If we crammed too many areas close together and then tried to cram in the radiographers afterwards, we would breach all the international protocols on the safe use of radiation and the required metres of radius around it. As the 'virtual autopsy' via computerised tomography (CT) scan has grown in popularity, we have had to find ways to squeeze in the enormous machinery somewhere.

I always think carefully about the role of the APTs, the Anatomical Pathology Technologists, who assist the pathologists in carrying out post-mortems but do many other things besides. They are often overlooked but are indispensable and at the core of a well-run mortuary. APTs pass instruments such as scalpels to pathologists and take the tissue samples. They weigh the organs as they are removed from a body and are essential for record-keeping. After a post-mortem, an APT will help to reconstruct and clean the body ready for storage or release to an undertaker. They will also be responsible for the day-to-day running of the mortuary service and are vital to ensure compliance with legislation and human tissue arrangements in the relevant jurisdiction. They receive the bodies into the mortuary and then on into body storage and track both the bodies and all of the property and samples stored. Almost all APTs that I have encountered have a particularly heightened sense of right and wrong. It is no surprise to me that it is thanks to them that many human tissue and health and safety scandals have been exposed and then righted. I build and strengthen their role into every disaster mortuary plan I write.

One of my first jobs in the gymnasium was to hold the tape measure for a radiographer as she marked out the exclusion zone for radiation around a white plastic scanning unit. We trialled a new approach in the UK for the Iraq deceased because their bodies were so likely to be affected by metal and munitions. The forensic team agreed that scanning for bullets and shrapnel would be the first stage when the mortuary received a body.

We put everything in place and then it was quiet for the first few days. While we waited for men and women to start dying, I watched from an upstairs window as the soldiers rehearsed lifting coffins off the Hercules plane used to repatriate the dead. We had used five or six large sandbags to replicate the weight of a body, organised into the shape of a head, and a torso and

legs. The pall bearers' shoulders shook with the weight
of the lead linings – standard for transporting bodies
by air – that I had sourced for the coffins of their
comrades. A few weeks later, we would repatriate
actual sand from the Iraqi desert, stained red with
blood. It had been gathered by collection teams
attempting to bring back whatever fragments they
could.

When we finally had word that the bodies of the
first conflict deceased might begin arriving soon, I
started to make preparations with funeral directors
for the next day. We started the preparations at 4.30
a.m., the soldiers carrying out one last rehearsal with
the coffins. After three hours, everyone was hungry,
so I led them to the base canteen for a full English
breakfast. They reached for their plates and trays.
Only then did I notice that the cavernous room was
now quiet. There was a thick and terrible silence as I
escorted sixteen funeral directors in full funereal dress
uniform of coat, tails and hat into a place where young
men and women were eating a last meal before boarding a military craft to the desert.

After a week of waiting, the bodies started to come.
Some came back in fragments but we repatriated a
number of men who seemed almost to be asleep.
Their repatriation from battle was so swift and the
temperatures used for cooling so effective that they
did not even look changed by the earliest stages of
decomposition. We learned that often those who were
untouched by bullet or improvised explosive device
(IED) had died from heatstroke, boiled alive in their

kits. Others had taken a small selection of ceramic plates out of their body armour to make them lighter in the heat and then been fatally shot through the gap. We repatriated the six 'Red Cap' military police killed by an Iraqi mob. Their bodies bore the signs of beatings with rifle butts and multiple bullet wounds. The bruising to their bodies suggested some of them were kneeling or lying on the floor when multiple final shots were fired at them.

Some of the coffins we were repatriating contained nothing more than a jumble of mismatching limbs from more than one person. They would be brought off the aircraft after all the other ceremonial exits, with the other coffins, had taken place. The sudden, powerful explosions of IEDs in Iraq and Afghanistan led to many amputations to the limbs of service personnel, some of whom lived and some did not. New self-applying tourniquets were now issued to all soldiers. When you apply a tourniquet you are making a decision – slowing the loss of vital blood from the body by sacrificing one or more parts of it. Sometimes the limbs would then be thrown further away into the sand, protected from fire and recoverable, so would be all we had to return. Soldiers who in all previous conflicts would have died in the field, lived. The original military risk assessments for Iraq did not plan for this. They expected more bodies, hence the body bags in the fax. What they got was limbless veterans instead, veterans whose lives were profoundly altered and would require years and years of support that had not been properly planned for.

I wanted to be present in the mortuary as much as possible, to see what was working, to ensure protocols were followed and to adapt things if necessary. There were usually four or five of us from Kenyon present and it was reassuring that Alan was one of the team. One of my jobs was to sort out the limbs. I would spend hours with these arms and legs. Six or eight at a time. Some of the coffins would only have feet in them. The first time the heavy lid was prised open, we all collectively took a step back and there were a series of low whistles and intakes of breath. I noticed Alan look over at me protectively. With Kenyon, you were thrown in fast and deep. You learned on the job. Alan was an experienced funeral director, with a speciality in complex cases and repatriations but he knew I had never seen anything like this. Though nor had he.

Some of the feet still had shoes on them: big, incongruous tan-coloured desert boots. Some of these feet were blistered and bleeding, shod in boots two sizes too small with another name sharpied onto the leather. The military liaison told me the UK soldiers didn't have boots suitable for the desert heat and conditions and would sometimes buy spare pairs from the American soldiers, even if they didn't fit. I have never been able to put out of my mind that they were sent to war without the boots that they needed.

Feet were more common but often it was hands too. Sometimes, with hands, if both the thumb and the little finger were damaged I would struggle to know if it was right or left. I was caught by my colleague, holding them up, turning them over and double-checking. I generally hid aspects of my dyspraxia well, such as my total inability to process right and left. But here it was a little more obvious. My colleagues pranked me by writing 'R' and 'L' on my shoes and overalls and placed two right-footed shoes by my locker.

At one time, the limbs might have been buried at the scene or incinerated without further comment. But the world had changed and this time they would be DNA tested. Even before 9/11, the president of the USA, George W. Bush, had instigated an international programme of bringing home the Second World War dead from sites all across the Pacific. No American would be left unknown. In the UK too, DNA testing in death was our new toy, with one coroner writing to the home secretary to complain that we had let a genie out of a bottle over which we had no control.

Once the DNA results for the limbs were in, I made arrangements for them to be reunited with the deceased in the UK and US. If the DNA tests came back and showed the limbs were those of the living – with no use for them now – they were sent for medical incineration. Two years later, after the 7/7 terrorist attacks, the Metropolitan police began to allow survivors to say goodbye to their limbs, arranging viewings of pieces and parts for survivors as well as the bereaved. Some of the police muttered darkly that this had all gone a bit far. But who are we to censor what works for healing? When my dad cut off his finger on a bandsaw, the doctors agreed no reattachment was possible. The nurses brought it out to him, he wished it well and bid it a fond farewell before it was taken to the hospital incinerator.

In Brize Norton, the feet were the major topic of conversation in a badly lit bar area that the base had made available just to us. A sole barman served us with flat, sweet Coca-Cola for me and whiskey for the drinkers, and let us order in Chinese takeaways at 10 p.m. This was the one safe space where the words would form. We were the dark secret on site, on an airbase where men and women were training daily to fly into war and it certainly would not have been ideal for them to see us sat back with a drink chewing over the events of the day. 'How's your day been?' my mum would enquire fondly, on a quick call. 'It's good, yeah, fine. Um, busy,' is all I could say.

Many of the experienced funeral directors were finding themselves in a brave new world where families were asking, demanding, for more rights and access than before. In the past, families had been made to feel abnormal for requesting access to a body or even the disaster scene itself. Pam Dix, writing about the experience of losing her brother in Pan Am flight 103 over the Scottish town of Lockerbie has written about being made to feel like a 'ghoulish sightseer' when she asked to visit the place where her brother's body had been found. A scene that then-Prime Minister Margaret Thatcher had already been allowed access to as a VIP guest.

Often my role was to arrange the logistics of a viewing of a body or a partial body. This was after we had formal identification through scientific testing, so was

purely for an emotional goodbye. The face thick with
embalmer's foundation and a generous helping of
Atrixo hand cream to help the foundation stay on
under the lights of the room. Sometimes the viewing
room would smell strongly of instant coffee. The
embalmer's facial reconstruction kit was often overwhelmingly biased towards white skin and I was
appalled to see that well into the 2000s the way round
this was to mix Nescafé granules into the mixture if
the deceased was anything other than pink. I was
heartened to hear recently about a new drive in the
manufacture of embalming, cosmetology and post-
death facial reconstruction make-up to ensure a
broader range of colours.

Responders and the wider public often assume that
families will want all signs of injury to be hidden but
that has rarely been my experience. Often they want
to feel and touch what they have been through. I have
watched mothers, fathers and partners trace the bullet
wounds and the bruising with the touch of a finger or
kiss the parts of the face that remain undamaged,
shedding tears into the ragged spaces where the
gaping wound begins.

I have learned that the use of cosmetology and
reconstruction is always a delicate balance – enough
to comfort but not too much as it will distress. I
soothed the aftermath of a colleague's assumption
early on in Brize Norton. A new widow was screaming, clawing at the face of her husband, infuriated that
his facial injuries had been covered up with 'make-
up'. And worse, that we had hidden the fatal injuries

to his neck with a ruff. 'He's a fucking soldier,' she screamed, 'and you've made him look like a fucking choirboy.' I train people to ask first now, which requires an honesty that many are still uncomfortable with when it comes to death.

A similarly delicate balance had to be found with the soldiers' belongings. We were instructed to clean letters of any soiling, without family permission, and then to laminate them. So heat seal them in hard plastic. The letters, often smuggled into undergarments or uniform against regulations, were damp with blood and body fluids. I would first sponge them off and dry them out on a grid of wire and wood. One of the ATPs with flowing locks lent me her Revlon hairdryer and I would sit and blow dry the letters with it on its lowest setting. This act of gently going back and forth with the hairdryer meant that I not only read the letters but heat seared them into my brain. Most were a mix of family news, tender love and then the kind of talk common between a husband and wife who are missing each other a lot. I remember the phrases within them to this day. And I found I could never use them with Tom again.

I felt initially outraged about the laminating, that we would render these letters hard and plastic, with sharp edges. The commanders had surmised that placing them in the plastic pocket would stop the transfer of any pathogens. It seemed excessive to me and ironic that the ministry would worry about that aspect when often the reason that the man was dead in the first place was their woeful management of his risks. And what if a widow wanted to fold it up and keep the letter close, I mused?

A few weeks after we conducted the return of the first batch of letters, I managed to escape work a little earlier and join Tom for a gym induction session. This was not my spiritual home but the pool did look lovely. As the fitness trainer was showing me how to use the treadmill, an image filled the TV screens that were dotted liberally around the whole space. They were tuned to local news and the newscaster was interviewing a woman recently widowed by the conflict. As I fumbled with the speed control buttons, she held up her laminated letter and her words reverberated around the space. She was expressing gratitude that she now knew he had received her last letter and had her words of love with him when he died.

A decade later I saw the same woman in a documentary commemorating ten years since the invasion of Iraq. I noticed she was still able to hold up her letter for the camera and read from it. She talked about how much she treasured it. Without the decision to laminate it, maybe it would have frayed into nothing long before.

The TV news blared constantly at work. It had been through the journalist Terry Lloyd's coverage that, on 21 March 2003, we learned things had ramped up significantly. The Iraqi military had been pushed back and were heading north. It would turn out to be Lloyd's last report.

The day after, Lloyd and his team tried to push forward towards Basra. Attempting to get the real story, away from the military propaganda, he had ended up beyond the frontline between Iraqi military and US military. The initial report was that Lloyd had ended up in hostile Iraqi territory and shot by the enemy. His body was identified by his friend and fellow journalist Trevor McDonald. The bodies of his cameraman and his translator were missing.[16]

Terry Lloyd was repatriated to us at Brize Norton. The newspapers were filled with his photograph and also pictures of his young son and daughter. I took charge of the arrangements. When his body arrived, I felt a protectiveness and a mourning I had no right to claim. Terry was managed separately in the mortuary from the other military repatriations. This was to be expected because he was a journalist and not a soldier but in my imagination, it was as though he was somehow being blamed for risk-taking and kept apart from his countrymen. I appreciated his bravery and his truth-seeking, and struggled to fathom that the man on our mortuary table was someone who had been such a regular in broadcasts watched in our family sitting room over the years.

As the pathologist worked, David Mannion, Terry and Trevor's friend and editor at ITN, waited outside in the corridors. ITN had wanted to send their own pathology representation but this was prevented under coronial law. Other news agencies and politicians were speculating that Terry's death was ITN's fault and therefore David's, as his editor. A few times,

I was sent to make him a cup of tea and said almost nothing to him. I was self-conscious in part because the horror of my beverages was legendary at that time – it was years before a kindly colleague took me in hand and explained you had to leave the teabag in the cup for a little while before adding the milk.

During the post-mortem, I was working nearby when our mild-mannered pathologist suddenly stopped his work and muttered, 'Fuck, fuck, fuck.' He released the bullets he found in Terry's body from his metal tweezers into a metal kidney dish. To those around the mortuary table, it was becoming clear that something did not fit with what we'd been told; the bullets told a different story. Terry had received multiple injuries at different times and it would later be shown that they were from American fire in a second incident. He hadn't been killed by Iraqi 'baddies'; in fact, we discovered later that Iraqi civilians had rescued him after he was caught in crossfire between American and Iraqi troops, sustaining a gunshot wound to the shoulder and a minor injury on his leg, which had been wrapped in a dirty bandage. He had been on the way to get help for survivable injuries when the American military ordered an attack on his convoy. Although the vehicles were clearly marked ITN and Press, officers later stated that they believe these vehicles to be hijacked and about to be used for a suicide bombing, so they had taken them out.

For three years this information was *sub judice*, 'under judgement' in court, and therefore not to be discussed elsewhere. I am often asked now what I find difficult about this work, with the assumption that it will be bodies or smells or scenes. But one thing that is distressing, is carrying around these toxic nuggets of knowledge, the future hurts. Stories like Terry's that must be concealed, even from your own family, until they have been properly aired to a court. So this weight lived in my brain and on my shoulders until finally, after thirty-six months, it was confirmed at the inquest that US Marines had fired on civilians in a minibus that was driving away from the firefight to get help for Terry's initial injuries and an unlawful killing verdict was returned.

A decade later, the Marines who fired on the minibus would be interviewed by Terry Lloyd's daughter for a documentary. The soldiers were haunted by what had happened. They recounted the chaos. There was a lack of clarity over where shots were coming from and a blurred frontline. There was confusion about who was on the minibus and concern that a missile was about to be launched from it.

There will always be multiple experiences of a sudden death and a hundred narratives of the same timeframe.

Many years after the Iraq war, in their new retirement bungalow on the Welsh border, my parents decided to have their roof repaired. A local lad who had set up a company after leaving the army provided a fair quote. My dad can make anyone talk. During several weeks up a ladder and through a steady stream of tea, digestive biscuits and apple turnovers, the lad unloaded to my dad about his best times and his worst times. Heady missions in Iraq and Afghanistan. My dad, with his love of Lee Child and Tom Clancy novels, absorbed all the gore and all the details.

There was one thing he would never get over, he said. His time in the Brize Norton mortuary. He was a munitions specialist, and had been asked to stand over the body of his best friend as his commanding officers asked him to identify the bullets that they were extracting. He had felt his legs go. The shame of fainting in front of his officers. He told my dad he had been caught by a young woman. Big tits. She got him outside and made him an awful cup of tea. He would never forget that girl, he said.

My dad thought no more of it until one hot August day I stepped out of the car to make a visit. The lad stumbled on the bottom rung of the ladder and all colour drained from his face. For the second time, I caught him. Neither of us spoke as he got in his van and drove away.

He sent his invoice by post.

4

Boxing Day

It was the morning after Christmas Day, 2004. I pulled on my new fleecy pyjamas and headed downstairs in Tom's family home, breathing air filled with the smell of cooking breakfast and festive spices. The television was on in the sitting room showing 'breaking news'. Wobbly, lopsided footage of a movie-sized wave with a soundtrack of screaming. Aftermath images of houses broken into sticks, cars wedged into trees. I stood transfixed. This looked very, very big.

Slowly it became clear that a tsunami had struck at 7.58 a.m. local time across fourteen countries, triggered by a massive undersea earthquake in the Indian Ocean, between the Burma and Indian tectonic plates. Later it would be defined as one of the deadliest natural disasters ever recorded. Tens of thousands of people were killed across Indonesia, Sri Lanka, India and Thailand.

'Turn it off,' Tom whispered hurriedly, rolling his eyes at seeing my attention fixed on an unfolding disaster *again*. It was killing the mood of a family

Christmas. I took a cup of tea, excused myself to the bathroom and waited for my phone to start ringing.

I had recently left Kenyon for both an academic position and a job in risk management for Cambridge City Council. I had successfully completed my master's degree. So now I was working on my ultimate dream: building up a small, solo consultancy through which businesses, governmental bodies or organisations of any shape or form could contact me for advice at any stage of any incident. They might call me beforehand, to develop plans and training, on the day it happened or one year later for a review and preparation for the next time. I charged a small fee for training, review and travel but took no fees during the initial incident.

Although disaster planning had been around for decades, our profession was only really starting to take shape and become more formally involved with government.[17] The key departments that manage running the country, the Home Office and Cabinet Office, as well as the Foreign and Commonwealth Office, had taken to bringing me in as an adviser. On 26 December 2004, my first call came from a young civil servant who had been told that I might know where to get some body storage units.

I had first forged strong connections with the Foreign Office in 2002 early in my time with Kenyon when three bombs had detonated on the island of Bali, killing 202 people, of whom 23 were British. The fatalities occurred when a backpack carried by a suicide bomber and also a large car bomb were detonated in an area called Kuta, which was packed with tourists enjoying the nightlife.

The UK government sent a small number of pathologists, APTs, anthropologists, detectives and dentists to the aftermath of the Bali bombing. It was my job to wait for the deceased back at Heathrow. There had been an undignified tussle behind the scenes as some senior civil servants back in Whitehall didn't think the government should pay for the deceased to be repatriated. Some of the British dead had no travel insurance and there was concern that if the government picked up the tab then future holidaymakers would have no motivation to get insurance. All the time that the government squabbled over this, the fragmented bodies deteriorated further. The team in Bali were in a state of growing distress. The bodies were decomposing in front of them and they needed the go-ahead to start getting them home. We offered our services pro bono. The situation was so bad that our Australian counterparts, also repatriating their own dead, had offered to step in and take care of the bodies for free.[18] From a diplomatic point of view, our government would not accept that.

Every minute of wrangling in the corridors of Westminster equated to further deterioration in the bodies of loved ones in Bali. It rendered the person lost a little further away from their human form. It's always a delicate balancing act between rushing to get the body back before further decomposition occurs and making unfixable errors with identification. The balance is almost impossible to achieve but we are always too slow. After three weeks of political stalemate, funding was granted for us to get the bodies home and into a temporary mortuary, via Heathrow. And I had to ensure they all came back.

Before the flight that was transporting the bodies landed, Tom and I had decided to grab a trip to the Science Museum and maybe lunch. This was our first time together for over a week – I had been working day and night on the repatriations and he was based in Ireland with his new aviation job. Almost as soon as we walked through the doors of the museum, my phone started to ring. As children and their parents swarmed excitedly around me at the human body exhibit, all ginormous pumping lungs and light up hearts, I stepped into a stairwell to hear that one of the coffins had gone missing.

Leaving Tom in the museum on his own with a flurry of apologies I caught a Piccadilly line tube train to Heathrow. It was the longest journey of my life. I ran through various terrible scenarios in my head and the terror turned my bowels to liquid. By the time I arrived, the missing coffin had been located. It was a simple administration error and the coffin had simply been moved to the wrong area.

When something terrible happens, the role of a disaster planner who has seen all this before is often, in the earliest stages, to act as a soothing balm. To remind the headless chickens around them that this will be OK – 'You got this.' The very first part of any disaster plan that deals with the deceased must establish how they will be gathered together, stored and protected so that the next stages of the work can begin. Bodies in the open air not only decompose but offend our human sensibilities and our sense of what it is to be civilised. So the first task in the management of the dead is to tidy them into refrigerated units.

Those first calls after the tsunami were about sense-making and placing some sort of net of order over the horror. There were practical issues to attend to. I pulled together a list of needed items to store the bodies, many of which were the same sorts of containers that our fruit and veg arrive in, but many had already been requisitioned locally by other nations looking for the same thing. Later I realised I could never have been fast enough for the conditions out there. Those images on my television screen that Boxing Day morning – dirty brown water, splintered houses, boats halfway up main roads and lots and lots of bodies – would become one of the largest and most wide-ranging disasters the world had seen. It was the biggest multi-nation 'mass fatality' operation ever attempted, to this day. And it threw up a fleet of problems. The UK teams and scientists that responded to some of the over 230,000 dead[19] were met with scenes and conditions that they had never encountered. I say *some of* the dead because in the days after the disaster, jostling teams from around the Western world headed in to try to retrieve and repatriate their bodies. Dead from the local communities were often not identified but buried in mass graves or cremated with others. There was little time or inclination to focus on cause of death, with drowning used as a blanket cause even when there was evidence of amputation of limbs or massive head trauma.

When police and scientists arrived in Thailand to help identify and repatriate the bodies, there was often a three-hour, bone-crunching trek along dirt tracks to reach the Buddhist temples where many of the bodies had been dragged. Blocks of dry ice were placed on the deceased, whose faces were blackening with decomposition minute by minute. Frantic relatives searched crowded hospitals for their loved ones; handwritten lists were drawn up of hundreds and hundreds of displaced travellers and pinned to bulletin boards. Local people who came across the bodies of babies or toddlers would often place them on top of the body of the nearest woman, hoping they were reuniting mother and child. In some areas, the local responders would later bury a man, a woman and a child together in mass graves – a semblance of a family but no knowledge of whether they were actually kin. The British scientists and police were plunged into a race against time to get to these bodies before they were lost forever in mass graves.

In the aftermath of the tsunami, the rate of decomposition was like nothing previously seen by British responders. In the heat of the sun over the Indian Ocean, and after lengthy exposure to sea water, the bodies were decomposing as they watched. Most were ragged bits of flesh and human soup by the time they made it back to the UK.

*   *   *

Disaster death is never gentle or peaceful. The bodies are rarely unharmed and they are usually hard to identify. So one of the most important parts of the disaster plan is how to give them back their name. Visual identification (a family member looking at the body of their loved one or a response worker comparing the body to photographs for example) can be fraught with difficulty for any death but disasters add further complications.[20] Decomposition happens incredibly quickly. Bodies bloat; eyes milk over; skin starts to slip and change colour. Bodies become harder to tell apart and tags and labels can slide off. The wrong body can be taken from a tray and repatriated by another country.

My career has coincided with the development of the science and practices of disaster victim identification (DVI), which was revolutionised by Lord Justice Clarke's findings in his report into the handling of the deceased in the *Marchioness* disaster, published in 2001. This report laid the foundations for the way we treated the disaster dead from then on.

In 1989, fifty-one people had died when a dredging vessel collided with the *Marchioness* pleasure boat on the River Thames in London. Almost half of the *Marchioness* dead had their hands severed by the pathologist working for the Thames coroner – models' hands, a pianist's hands, a ballerina's hands. This was common practice in the 1980s for river dead as it is easier to fingerprint a severed hand after it has been in water. The outer layer of skin on the hand – the crucial part where the fingerprint pad sits – degloves.

Some pathologists will even pull on this glove over their own and make the fingerprints from over the top of their own fingers.

The pathologist assumed that somebody later would reattach those hands and hide the big stitches under puffy sleeves or a jacket but often they were just tucked under the body in the coffin. Some of the hands were found much later in a mortuary fridge. I attended an event for *Marchioness* families days after the coroner had supplied them with what was hopefully the final list of all those who had lost their hands, ten years after the disaster had happened. Many family members were pale with shock and distress. Some still have lingering doubts that the last list was accurate.

This was just one way in which the treatment of the disaster dead could amplify the suffering of families. Disaster Action had seen it over and over again: in the well-meaning lie told to Maureen Kavanagh that her son had been asleep at the moment of impact; in the order for *Marchioness* victim Shaun Lockwood-Croft's coffin to remain sealed. It contributed to his mother Margaret's ongoing belief that the body in the coffin was not Shaun. The body was later described in forensic papers as that of a bald man when her son had thick, black hair. She campaigns for his exhumation even now.

Lord Justice Clarke's report into the handling of the *Marchioness* disaster contained not only a detailed list of recommendations but also a set of overarching principles that should govern the response to a disaster. They are:

- Provision of honest and, as far as possible, accurate information at all times and at every stage
- Respect for the deceased and the bereaved
- A sympathetic and caring approach throughout
- The avoidance of mistaken identification.

Barristers for the families at the inquiry emphasised that those working behind the closed doors of the mortuary, away from the relatives' gaze, had a particular responsibility to care for the dead with respect. In the years to come, that report would become the lens through which I scrutinised everything I did. I joined a band of helpers of the unidentified dead who prided themselves on being 'Lord Clarke compliant'.

Following this report, the work of caring for the dead of disaster in the UK was transformed. We became world-leading in disaster victim identification (DVI). From then on, this work of identification would involve a team of specially trained police officers, with senior police officers assigned to oversee the gathering of evidence as directed by the coroner. They would work alongside pathologists (flesh), anthropologists (bones) and forensic odontologists (teeth) to identify the dead. To get them the evidence they need, they would be aided by APTs and radiographers. Later, DNA scientists would also be added into the mix. There can be hundreds of people working inside a disaster mortuary.

The post-mortem side of disaster victim identification is only one side of the story, however. Along with the work that is carried out at the mortuary, police officers trained as family liaison officers deploy to gather evidence from family members. The role is often mistaken as one of just family support but they have a specific role to investigate and act as a link between the wider investigation and the family. The police FLOs go to great personal lengths, often working all hours, to be available to the families to receive and pass on information relating to the investigation. They are tasked to complete a lengthy ante-mortem form with the families, gathering intensely detailed and personal information on the dead. It is called ante-mortem, 'before death', because it relates to details about their loved one before the incident. The whole procedure is rather brutally referred to in police training as the 'ante-mortem harvest' and, because of the intimate nature of the questions, has been significantly controversial among families.

Over twenty pages long, the form asks about descriptions of the nose (alcoholic?), the ears (prominent?), pubic hair design (trimmed, jewellery?), tattoos, one leg shorter than the other. These forms are a legacy of the days when Interpol would respond to major transport disasters by matching a family's description of the anatomy to a torso or limbs in the mortuary. They work for bodies that are strictly binary – only accommodating male or female biological sex – and there have been a number of occasions when transgender bodies have confounded responders. (If all that is recovered from a crash scene is some tissue, vertebrae, trachea and a pelvis, none of these can be changed by drugs or surgery – the recovered remains will be recorded initially as their biological sex, not by the identity of the deceased in life.) These forms are meant to be completed at some of the worst moments of a family member's life. Relatives may still be clinging on to hope that their loved one never boarded the flight or cancelled their shopping trip after all. But they must still wrack their brains for every tiny physical anomaly on their frame.

This ante-mortem data is collected on forms printed on yellow paper. It is matched to the post-mortem data printed on pink paper. It is then taken to an Identification Commission made up of the coroner, forensic specialists and the police senior identification manager (SIM), who formalise the confirmation of identities. Despite the grand-sounding name, the commission is just a meeting at police headquarters or in a town hall. The process implies that an identity is something separate from the body itself. It can be given and taken away and can be correct or incorrect. All of this can take a long time and add to the family's woes.

I have seen mistakes with identification occur with just a single deceased and confusion between the deceased occur with as few as two bodies, or one survivor and one deceased. I have learned to spot the incidents where we need to be extra cautious. I have been called for advice where there are three generations of one family in a motorway pile-up. Or a hen-do of young women, the mother of the bride, two aunties, with everyone wearing the same neon pink t-shirt, their relationship to the bride embroidered in plastic crystals across the shoulder blades. On 6 April 2018, I saw TV reports of a fatal bus crash involving the Humboldt Broncos junior hockey team on their way to the play-offs in the Saskatchewan league. I noticed that the photos showed a group of young men who were physiologically very similar. They had the same kit on and, in an extra twist of fate, they had *all* dyed their hair canary yellow for the game. In spite of the care that I knew the Canadian DVI teams would take, this would be almost impossible to get right. Sure enough, the first notification of a misidentification error came to families on the Sunday night, forty-eight hours later. A young man whose family had been told was dead was actually alive in hospital. Another man was not in critical care as his family hoped but in the mortuary.

Tiny mistakes are made almost every day, that are hopefully caught before they result in the release of a wrongly identified body. I have made a few myself. I have seen labels accidentally switched or washed off, two forms mixed up together, samples put into the wrong bag. In some inquiries into the actions of police and scientists, families have interpreted these errors as hugely significant signs of conspiracy. Sometimes they are but in my experience they are more likely the result of a slip of a biro or a muddled, tired head. We build into the plan as many checks and balances as we can.

To understand why mistakes in identification occur in disaster settings, you really need to have spent time with the deceased of disaster. At the scene, sometimes it can be hard to work out what was once part of a living person. Even intact and undamaged bodies are changed by sea water or exposure to the sun. Faces sink inwards, eyes change colour. Cognitive bias and assumption also creep in. When the King's Cross Underground fire in 1987 claimed thirty-one souls, the majority were identified by relatives. The police then looked to the personal effects and particularly the jewellery. In the mortuary, the pathologist had declared one of the unidentified deceased a white male. At the same time, the mother of John Fitzgerald St Prix was reporting him missing. John was black and he had been wearing gold jewellery. John's mother was told none of the remaining deceased matched her son's description. It was almost a month later when Mrs St Prix's fears were confirmed using fingerprint comparison. There had been confusion. His skin had been altered to appear white by the fire, they told her. And the descriptions of the gold jewellery had been of no use because the gold had melted beyond recognition in the heat.

In circumstances such as road deaths or death in hospital, the coroner may decide that identification through viewing by family members is sufficient. Identifiers such as distinctive jewellery, scars, marks, tattoos, amputations, medical records, X-rays or the presence of ID badges are considered supporting 'secondary' sources. But for the dead in larger incidents and disasters, the preferred options are 'primary' sources, such as fingerprints, dental records, DNA and possibly medical identifiers such as hip replacements and breast implants.[21]

Teeth are most popular as the initial positive identifier, as they are resistant and likely to be preserved intact even when the rest of the body is in a bad state. They are also a part of our body that is regularly examined and charted. The forensic odontologist matches the jaw and the teeth on the body before them to a set of paper or electronic records. However, it is not always possible to get dental records for the dead. The slaves working in a city centre nail bar don't usually have a dental plan, for example. It is believed that thousands of undocumented workers were buried without an identity after the tsunami. But while teeth may be an identifier that accompanies privilege, ironically having a good dentist can also create its own problems. So much of our dentition is now so good and so uniform that we have stripped our mouths of a map for the odonts to follow. But we still tend to go with teeth first in the UK.

The combination of Lord Clarke's report in 2001 and the effects of responding to the tsunami in 2004 galvanised the scientists, mortuary staff and police who were tasked with caring for the UK's disaster dead. Not all countries developed the same approach and following an international incident like the tsunami, there is still a rush to get to the British citizens first, before other nations start removing the hands and the jaws, for example. When the British dead of the Indian Ocean tsunami had started to be returned to the UK in 2005, the coroner had to issue an apology for the removal of these body parts by other international DVI teams.

In a battle of tsunami versus human endeavour, the sheer breathtaking power of the destruction was always going to outnumber any efforts on the ground to identify the dead. But watching the teams return to the UK with a zeal to improve the care of the dead and of their families confirmed my growing belief that I had joined the field at its most exciting and innovating time. To lay hands on the body one last time, to gather what could be found and to try to give that person a name felt like the most important work I could be doing.

5

Forty-four Minutes of Chaos

On the morning of Tuesday 7 July 2005, I was in London, running late for a meeting about caring for people after emergencies that was to take place in Whitehall. Emergency planning was buzzing with excitement and energy and the obvious place to focus much of our work was on the nation's capital city. It was exactly one week after our national emergency planners' conference, where we had focused on the risks and threats facing our country at the time, including a session on the implications of a mass evacuation of the entire London Underground network.

I got on the tube at Rayners Lane station, on the Piccadilly line, thirty minutes after I'd meant to. I had been staying with a friend who had a new baby and I had held him and smelt his hair long enough to make me late. Our train ground to an unscheduled stop just after 9 a.m. We sat in silence and then I noticed Underground staff moving at pace – not running, but faces set to action mode.

About twenty minutes later, I was being evacuated at a station I didn't know by a policeman who was screaming at the top of his lungs. He seemed young and panicked. I watched him roughly grab an old man in robes, with a beard, who was taking too long to shuffle down the carriage, while he screamed at him, 'Fucking move! Because out there, people are fucking dying.'

The policeman's hostility towards this man and a strange message about 'no networks available' on my Nokia 3210 told me everything I needed to know. This was the threat we had been planning for in the UK ever since 9/11. An improvised explosive device attached to a vest or within a rucksack of a man or woman willing to die for their cause. It had been deployed effectively in so many other countries and we knew it was coming here. It had *always* been a question of when. As we were herded out of the station, I realised the notes on planning for just such an event were in my rucksack; I just had not expected to be on this side of the fence.

Frontline responders within the Underground network were not as well briefed as me on these threats. At a debrief a few weeks later, we were played the transmissions from the scene and it was clear that some Underground workers initially thought this was something to do with the electrics. A series of not-uncommon power surges on the lines that would result in smoke and sparks and a few hours of minor disruption. But we could hear the tone on the recordings change abruptly when the injured start to appear. Several of them were so badly damaged that their families did not recognise them in hospital.

The coroner for the inquest into the deaths on 7 July 2005 described 'forty-four minutes of chaos' in the immediate aftermath of three suicide bombers almost simultaneously blowing themselves up on three Underground trains across the London network. A fourth bomber detonated his bomb on a red London bus in Tavistock Square, his initial plan to also blow up a train thwarted. The damage the bomber did there stained the white walls of the British Medical Association building salmon pink, until somebody ordered them washed and repainted. The twisted frame of the bus became a totemic image of the attacks. The poles that commuters routinely cling onto when drivers negotiate difficult corners stuck out at all angles and left a particular type of bruising down the middle of some survivors' faces. Media organisations and conference organisers used the images liberally. A London bus for a London attack. The untrained eye doesn't realise that there are still identifiable bits of person in those images. Broadcasters make the same mistakes sometimes with footage of plane crashes and scenes of conflict.

Some aspects of the media seized on the coroner's description of forty-four minutes of chaos as a criticism of the responders. But the fact it had been just forty-four was a bloody miracle. The initial response is always frenzied and brain-numbingly overwhelming. A terrorist attack was a completely predictable risk for London and emergency plans had been written for it – plans that tell people where to go, what to say and what to bring with them. But that does not mean there won't be chaos once you factor in the vagaries of human behaviour and the collision of an unusual set of circumstances.

Older planners with a military background like to use the phrase 'the plan rarely survives first contact with the enemy'. There is truth in this but the admission of defeat also frustrates me. No one expects the disaster plans we develop to flow perfectly when they meet reality but, nonetheless, they serve many important functions and provide a stabilising influence on shaking hands. Disaster plans help us to alert incident commanders of what they need to do before they even know such problems exist. Even seasoned responders will be fogged by cortisol and adrenaline in the early stages of a major incident. On a clipboard or an electronic tablet, the plans give us something to hold on to, a psychological device to clarify thoughts and focus. They can be as simple as a checklist of key actions but it allows the eyes to focus in on things that need to be done and an order in which to do them. Moving people. Bringing in resources. Applications for no-fly zones to thwart the news helicopter and, in more recent years, the news drones.

A more intractable problem is that the people turning up to enact the plan's dot-to-dot sequences are often the most senior commanders in the area. We call it the moment that 'the scrambled eggs have landed', a reference to the curly twill on the commanders' epaulettes, which looks a bit like breakfast. When the call comes in, the commanders want a piece of the action but rarely have they engaged in the vital and most recent training or exercises, so they often get it wrong.

The London Underground, as its name suggests, is largely below ground in the centre of the city, which meant that access could be easily controlled by fire, police, ambulance and forensic teams on what would soon become known in disaster shorthand as 7/7. The scenes brought their own myriad of operational challenges, however – like rodents, terrible air and asbestos. After the Russell Square bomb, the police and paramedics had to walk for over twenty minutes in full breathing apparatus, in almost complete darkness, carrying all their equipment to even be able to attempt a rescue. The bus bombing presented different challenges for responders. The bus was cleaved open and visible. The comings and goings could be seen by all.

One of the first and biggest problems at the site of the bus bomb was something I had seen before – pigeons. Since my work on 9/11, pigeons had been a high alert on my radar. I was tasked with finding teams to be sent to New York to clear the bird nests and guttering in some of the buildings surrounding Ground Zero. It seemed that pigeons and other birds were scooping up the smallest human bones, the finger bones or *phalanges,* that were still being uncovered at the site and building them into the fabric of their nests. A pinky bone in a pigeon's nest could be all that was left of someone from the World Trade Center and the key to unlocking their identity. These bones needed to be recovered and tested for DNA.

Many of the bones discovered were not human but came from catering services. There were twenty-two restaurants in the World Trade Center, plus grocery shops and office kitchens. And workers' packed lunches. A large anthropology team worked for years separating these out, alongside technologists working in the new field of DNA. We sent the New York medical examiner our best mortuary teams to supplement their own. And this left me with a permanent passion for protecting tiny bones at scenes. And a wariness of pigeons.

One of the first lines in the plan for an open scene like the bus bombing was to deploy a hawk to keep the pigeons away. They called in the one that they had on a contract for the Wimbledon tennis tournament every year. The pigeons hated it. One week after the bombs, the London mayor's office received a complaint from animal rights campaigners about the hawk. The senior identification manager had to leave the ongoing work to recover and examine the bodies from four scenes to reassure the mayor's office that the hawk was only scaring the pigeons, not eating them.

Meanwhile, the remains needed a mortuary.

I was not thinking about most of this on the morning of 7/7 when I, and my fellow travellers, were taken to a nearby public library and told we could use the landline to phone another landline. I could not remember any landline numbers. Local authorities had specific recovery spaces ready to go but I found out later from colleagues that people were just directed to any available building. This is common in disaster. The police commandeer schools and libraries that are not the designated space, much to the planners' frustration. We stumble towards the place that has lights on, a tea urn and a smiling face, regardless of whether it is part of the official disaster plan.

I really only developed a true sense of events at debriefs weeks later. For now, I could tell that in the disaster hierarchy, we evacuees were low down on the pecking order. No immediate risk to our lives. No injuries. One of the librarians confirmed that something grave and life threatening was going on elsewhere but nobody knew quite what that was. In later years, I would hear such refugees from a chaotic situation describe themselves as 'survivors'. But we were bystanders. Our plans for the day were scuppered but ultimately we could go about our business, albeit delayed: some of those evacuated were asked to stay in a nearby open space for almost seven hours.

On that morning all I wanted was to go home. Adrenaline coursed through me and was not improved by the knowledge of the plans in my backpack. 'Fight or flight' is a common immediate reaction to any traumatic event, drilled into our DNA from ancient times. Emergency plans usually include a rather fruitless attempt to thwart this most basic of human instincts and get people to wait, leave their contact details, give a full statement. While our bodies are screaming at us, with a rush of energising hormones, to get ourselves up and away. One of the most critically injured survivors from a recent incident only started to realise the effects of her near-fatal injuries after she had calmly called her husband, been driven home and started to make a cup of tea. Her injuries were found to be so severe that in later surgery, she lost her spleen.

In flight from the library all I wanted was to find Tom, 300 miles away, but no trains to the north would be possible from King's Cross or Euston. I caught a black cab to Heathrow. The driver and I agreed to pick up everyone who stuck their hand up on the way past. We filled up the cab. A few of us split the fare. The cab ride was filled with nervous laughter. I felt the heady taste of the euphoric, honeymoon stage in immediate disaster aftermath. Sitting a little too close together, glad to be alive. My fellow passengers marvelled at their newfound lust for life, ready to hug their wives and partners.

When it was just me and the driver left in the cab, he told me why he had been a bit wary when I had hurriedly jumped into the back of his cab, shouting, 'Heathrow please!' He had kept checking on me in the rear-view mirror. He explained that eighteen years earlier, he had been working outside the station on the night of the King's Cross fire when a man in a suit with a briefcase had leapt into his cab and demanded to go to Heathrow, too. 'I looked round,' he said, 'and he was a little bit on fire. I had to say to him, "Mate, you're on fire, I need to get you some help."' So he had been looking in the mirror, wondering if I was a little bit on fire too.

*   *   *

I was working as a consultant to both the Home Office
and the Cabinet Office when an agreed protocol for a
terrorist attack and 'mass fatalities plan' for all the
coroners within the capital had been signed off just
seven days before the attacks. A formidable stable of
forensic experts, senior coroners and senior police
officers had effectively lobbied the Home Office for a
professionalised and resourced national mortuary
service that could be deployed anywhere in the country. Now it was to be tested for the first time.

In London, the mortuary that was erected could
have cared for hundreds of deceased, possibly thousands.[22] The structure was procured from one of the
government's military contacts who supplied
demountable structures in Iraq and Afghanistan as
military bases. It was put up on the grass at the headquarters of the Honourable Artillery Company near
Old Street, which ruined the wedding plans of several
senior military planners' daughters. It had enough
capacity and kit to allow for separate areas for each of
the four bombing sites. There were offices, changing
rooms, rest areas, catering. A viewing chapel. Even a
space for a massage therapist, after the Metropolitan
police took advice on 'wellbeing'.

Humanitarian assistance centres are also needed
after disasters – places where families and victims can
receive information and support. One particular area
of advocacy by Disaster Action was to improve these
physical spaces. The first humanitarian assistance
centre for the 7/7 bereaved was hastily constructed in
a council leisure centre.[23] The location and the

acoustics were all wrong. When families started to cry as they received the worst news imaginable, the sounds echoed all around, bouncing off the walls. Plus the place smelt of swimming pools and Disaster Action were always hugely aware of olfactory trauma and memory too, and pointed out that going for a swim or to a hotel with a pool might be a way that a parent or a child would seek some respite in the months to come. It was a cruelty to add the smell of pool chlorine to their olfactory memory. The government minister Tessa Jowell took a brave decision that this was not the right place for the families. Disaster Action were used as trusted advisers for the new '7th July Humanitarian Assistance Centre' at the Royal Horticultural Halls near Victoria Station. It was the largest and longest running that had been attempted in the UK.

I remember every disaster by its personal effects. The aftermath of 7/7 was all about coats, bags and office workers' lunchboxes. Tupperware filled with salad, wallets, blown-off clothing and items of jewellery. Tourists' cameras, wheelie bags, laptops and the thick paper wodge of a near-to-submission PhD thesis, still being annotated up until the point that the bomb exploded. Paperback books to help pass the time on a lengthy and uncomfortable Underground journey, all twisted around bits of burnt rubber, seat upholstery and distorted metal. Spilling out of handbags were lipsticks, perfumes, Tampax. And watches, stopped, their faces cracked after impact. These small objects are often the source of substantial pain in the disaster aftermath, as families inevitably interpret that as a time of death.

I was asked to help advise on the handling of these items and I poured into that response every bit of learning I had from twenty different responses at Kenyon, as well as a hundred Disaster Action stories. The detective in charge of the personal effects was, fortunately, a great listener. The first principle I discussed with her and the police exhibits team was they should not make assumptions as to what property people may or may not want returned and in what state. It's a lesson that needs regularly repeating.

I made repeated visits to the warehouse where the effects were being stored and also the upper floors of the iconic New Scotland Yard building, with its shiny spinning sign, for meetings and briefings with the police. One of the most common assumptions from outsiders is that we are so much more slick and hi-tech than we actually are, and that there is a level of government rigour that will always kick in at the worst times.[24] I call this 'the *Skyfall* effect'. In the Daniel Craig era of James Bond movies, Bond works within a hugely impressive machine to keep Britain safe from hidden threats. He has 'M' and 'Q' and artificially intelligent cars and futuristic computer screens. He can get 'eyes' on London whenever he wants. But the reality of these spaces is dust bunnies on windowsills, a paper flip chart recording actions, a leak in the ceiling and a reminder to pay into the milk club and not leave your mugs in the sink.

I warned the detectives to expect the personal effects in waves. First come the items removed from the body itself at the mortuary, like stud earrings and wedding rings. They are often returned to the family in evidence bags or a plain cardboard box. British APTs are rigorous at removing and inventorying the items. The family may ask to keep them or they may ask for them to be replaced on the body and buried with them.

The next wave is often from the scene itself, luggage and rucksacks, mingled with cargo. There is also a category of objects that come from the DVI process itself and have to also be considered and returned. One of the first things that a family will be asked for as part of the ante-mortem harvest is exhibits from which the scientists can extract DNA or a fingerprint comparison. Toothbrushes, CD cases, baby teeth collected for the tooth fairy and, the one that got me somewhere deep in my gut, a set of tiny grubby foot-prints imprinted in a highchair tray. For the first time in a UK policing operation, following the 7/7 attacks, the detectives brought these exhibits that the families provided into the personal effects process too, taking the same care over the way they were returned.

The last items to be released to the families are those held onto by the policing and intelligence agencies. If it is a terrorist incident or an air crash, phones are normally retained as their contents can provide potentially crucial evidence. They are stored in what are called Faraday bags, clever little mesh pouches that block an external signal that might try to wipe their data. They may be returned much later or, in some cases, not at all. Sometimes items are held onto in error and found much later in a dusty evidence store or they are held while a criminal trial drags out for years. The families of the Lockerbie bombing in 1988 did not receive their items for over ten years; some had been almost completely destroyed by mould and mildew by the time they were given back.

I spent a lot of time with the 7/7 detectives working out the optimum conditions for storing and protecting these personal effects, helping them to avoid the traps waiting to grab at their ankles. One example was allowing for flexibility in terms of timings. It is a common reaction for families to want to wait and take time rather than comply with an external agency's timetable. A number of bereaved relatives felt unable to open the cardboard box of personal belongings to confirm that the contents matched with the restoration receipt they were required to sign. So we built in more time. We also offered choices to families upfront. Every family was asked about what they wanted to happen to every item. Necklaces that had glinted in the gloom of the tube carriage floor. A book that was blown from the hands of one young woman and used as a headrest by paramedics for another. The family of one victim wanted every item of clothes to be laundered, except the jeans. Their loved one hated the jeans being newly washed and crinkly, the parents said. So they got the jeans back 'as is'.

So many of the Disaster Action relatives had told me stories of over-enthusiastic laundering of their loved one's effects, without any recourse to asking them what they wanted. Stains that had been there long before the disaster and reminded someone of a pleasant memory had been scrubbed out. Tiny rips and scuffs that had been part of the jacket's pre-death history had been mended. I spoke to mothers of the dead at Hillsborough who were similarly distraught on learning that their sons' lucky shirt had been washed. They did not want it washed until they won the cup or the league.

During the Iraq war, I had turned up to a tense situation in the Kenyon warehouse in Bracknell. A new freelance team member, an older woman who was overzealous with the Brasso, had taken it upon herself to polish up a wedding ring, some dog tags and, devastatingly a St Christopher medal, that were in our care. They had been removed from what was left of a young soldier killed in an explosion. When it came to items of jewellery we *never* repaired or cleaned items without first gaining written family approval. I knew that the St Christopher, the patron saint of travellers, was an heirloom and that its patina would be part of that. It had belonged to a number of generations of military wearers. I was so horrified (and embarrassed, as I was in charge of the team) that I even briefly toyed with the idea of grubbying up the items in some way and hiding what had happened. But of course, we had to be honest with the families and they were particularly upset about the medal. Once the cleaning is done you can't get the dirt – life's patina – back.

Another question that the 7/7 detectives had was about censoring items and I was ready for that one too. Many of the young people killed and injured on that day had a mobile phone – then a reasonably new technology that had opened up new avenues for conducting personal relationships as they became more affordable and available. Me and Tom included. Much of our intimacy and connection was sustained by the sending of cheeky text messages when apart, late at night.

As expected, the decision had been taken by the counter-terror side of the investigation to retain the phones recovered from the scene. But they decided to allow the printing of data, once checked for intelligence secrets or evidence, within them onto lengthy documents. These would then be released to next of kin, who were usually the parents. This created an excruciating scenario where the early missives sent between second and third dates, as sexual tension built, were printed off and handed over to Mum and Dad. The detectives thought briefly about censoring these documents – or maybe even failing to hand them over altogether – but heard me out when I pointed out that this was simply not their role and liable to cause more distress. I knew also that those messages did something else for the bereaved: they showed that their relative had, until the moments of the tragedy, been living a life full of promise and excitement. There was comfort in that, amongst the terrible pain.

At Kenyon, discussions on censoring and also the management of any prohibited items were discussed early on with whoever was contracting us and the relevant law enforcement agencies. Illegal items, extreme pornography, drugs or weapons, would be carefully entered back into the investigative/policing side of business and we would hear no more. But some police forces and military units would also remove legal but 'racy' or controversial items, such as Viagra or condoms. When working with Islamic cultures on the lost planes of Middle Eastern airlines, the list of censored items was sometimes longer and might include swimming costumes, underwear and financial instruments such as chequebooks and debit cards.[25] Another common area for censorship, particularly by the military, was anything that gave away another life or another love that was perceived as less conventional at the time, such as letters from a boyfriend to a man. I fought hard against the removal of *Loaded* and *FHM* magazines, which were described by officials as 'like pornography'. I won and they were included in the returned items. I later discovered that sometimes it was the mothers who had bought their sons their subscription, hoping it would provide some light relief while they were in a conflict hellhole or stationed on an oil rig. They took comfort knowing that they had received their latest edition before they died. It is not for us to know, or decide, or prioritise, what will be important to a grieving mother, father, child, partner or wife.[26]

In a hot, windowless room I once watched a male police officer explain in a voice that a child would understand that the mobile phone casing on a dead man's phone was going to be destroyed. His family could however view a photograph of it. A photograph of the phone. Not the man. I knew that all we had of the man was fragments of burned tissue and one leg of a pair of suit trousers. The mobile phone had been in the pocket. The petite, beautiful lady opposite the policeman, half his size, whispered, 'Why?'

The officer stumbled and stammered about health and safety, protection. It was for her own good. All of a sudden, as if possessed by the strength of ten tigers, the woman in front of him grew straighter and taller in her chair. She was a senior scientist in a world-renowned forensic laboratory which had pioneered the science he was describing. He was trying to tell her, badly, that her husband's DNA, his blood, his life force might be on the phone. She understood and she still wanted it back. It was his. And now it was hers. She did not want it cleaned. She, better than this police officer in front of her, knew the risks of human pathogens contained in bodily fluids and how to safely manage them away. She would have the phone.

The policeman left the room cowed but still exacted one last vengeful humiliation. She would be made to sign multiple disclaimers saying that for her own safety she would never remove the phone from its plastic bag. I asked him why. 'Well, she might be batshit,' he opined. 'If we let her take it out of the bag she might try and clone him . . . She knows how.'

I think about the precious treasures that I have returned every day. It has changed my relationship with the objects in my life. When I pay with a credit or debit card, I run my finger over the raised numbers and remember all the times that one of the only things we could return was a bank card, the Mastercard or Visa logo still there, the edges black and charred. And other memories swim up every time I jangle keys or un-mat the hair of an Elsa doll or pull on jeans optimistically.

What do people do with the personal effects when we return them? For some survivors they become important artefacts – placing on a shelf the shoe that still bears the shrapnel marks or creating a textile picture made from the clothes they were wearing. While others, after the months of storage and some-times weeks of careful repair and laundering, simply throw the item away. It becomes too unbearable to retain. But families of the deceased are much more likely to keep them and take great comfort from them.

It is the text messages sent on the morning of 7 July 2005 that I think about most often. The conversations cut short in the middle of an argument or the middle of a new love affair or even just asking 'What's for tea?' Never meant to be seen by anyone other than the intended recipient.

The end of a thread of anger or lust, hope or dejection.

Love and life interrupted forever.

6

Hiraeth

The foul mix that enters under the doors and rises up under the skirting boards is more thick gravy than water. Everything about it feels dangerous and contaminating – dead rats, dead cats, engine oil, human turds and bits of loo paper – rushing at and into the house. As the rain doesn't stop, or the river-banks are too overwhelmed to do anything other than burst, residents might plead for sandbags and local authorities will often deliver them. Mainly as a placebo and a pacifier, knowing that apart from potentially a brief slowing down of the sludge's pace and possibly filtering out some of the shit, they are useless.

One of the things that always takes people by surprise is the speed of the water's ingress. Those who have never been flooded imagine you would have much more time to react, to move things upstairs, maybe. To carefully select the things that you want to save, cherish. But the destruction is usually fast. When talking about it later, I have noticed that people caught in floods always use a cutting gesture across the part of their body that represents where the water got to – sometimes up to their necks.

Professionally, for me, the first decade of the 2000s was a great time to be an emergency planner in the UK. Life was a heady rush of advising ministers and their teams, improving plans and helping people. I had meetings about innovating and improving the care of families after disaster, overhauled policy documents and ran conferences, while simultaneously tackling issues linked to safety culture. I was always busy.

I was well embedded into working with the Cabinet and Home Office, in part due to how seriously the government of the time took disaster planning. I had a university position and had also been approached to start teaching at the Emergency Planning College – the country's training hub for disaster work. I was often asked to arrange the learning and debrief events after disasters. Here we would pass on from planner to planner our lessons of what worked well when trouble hit.

In my personal life, things were going well, too. Tom and I had bought our first home together in Doncaster, a new build on land that had once been a coal mine, and we had been joined by our dog, Izzy. Tom was flying from nearby Doncaster Airport for a major airline. I set about making the house a home and finally I had somewhere to curate my clutter. Friends often describe our house as 'cosy' and 'lived in', which I interpret to mean full of crap. I keep almost everything: bus tickets from family days out, orders of services for weddings and funerals and old toys and books, alongside my piles of dusty boxes and decaying lever arch folders containing disaster plans past. And now that I was a home-owner, I would often treat myself to an interior design magazine and flirted with brightly coloured feature walls and a chintzy spare room for our visitors.

On 24 June 2007, about a year after we moved in, I was travelling back home from London by train. The rains had been doing their worst and the journey took several hours longer than it should have and resulted in a taxi for the final part. At one point, we were halted outside Peterborough due to 'swans on the line'. My fellow East Coast Main Line passengers and I watched as the swans were carried by rescuers in waterproofs before the train was allowed to continue on its voyage through this surreal landscape. Fields to our left and right were completely submerged, with cows and sheep swimming and water lapping at the edges of railway tracks. By the time I was back in Doncaster, a major incident was already underway.

Emergency planners spend a lot of time mapping out how the floods might come and then we share generic templates for what to do on the days themselves: mostly moving people to higher ground and into leisure centres and schools.

Many areas across Great Britain experienced severe flooding that June but South Yorkshire was particularly badly hit and forty-eight areas of the large borough of Doncaster were affected. Luckily, our house was high enough to escape the floodwaters but the disruption, the closed roads and evacuated houses were all around us. In the borough 3,286 homes were flooded with 2,275 suffering 'major damage'. The evacuation of the village of Toll Bar had gone on long into the night and had been terrifying.

Geographically, the village sits in a bowl that had essentially filled with water when a nearby river, the Ea Beck, burst. A large proportion of the village's housing was single-storey bungalows and they had disappeared under the waterline. The council had laid on buses but they were already full and had no wheelchair access. Many of the residents trudged through water and rain to get to the local leisure centre. Some of the local lads, known for causing trouble before the floods but now fast-tracked to sainthood for their actions that night, had found some boats and towed the older residents to safety. 'Nobody asked where the boats had come from,' the residents chuckled.

By the time I arrived at the centre, called in to advise on what next, people's clothes were already drying on makeshift racks, chairs, the handle of a baby's pram and the basketball hoops. The council purchased tracksuits from Asda for them to wear in the meantime. There was a lot of distress about the whereabouts of pets. The Fire and Rescue Service had already informed one family that their greyhound had been found dead in an outhouse.

I was often called in by local councils and Doncaster was a favourite, as well as being my new home. Before the floods, I had enjoyed talking at their local work-shops and helping them with their community risk register. This is a planning tool that we use to list and try and get ahead of local risks – chemical factories, rivers, a busy bus terminus. When the floods hit, they were keen to seek my advice on the long road ahead. Despite being in constant political turmoil, the local council had some of the most dedicated emergency planners and community engagement workers that I had ever encountered. In a situated disaster – a disaster of place – responders and residents are often entangled. Responders who came from the place, were born of the place, are often more fiercely protective of it and more interested in longer-term 'coming back' rather than just response.

Kenyon had trained me to take charge in settings like family assistance centres and repatriation cere-monies for short bursts of time-limited assistance. But it was here in Doncaster that I first learned about 'recovery listening', which mostly involved staying silent. A few nights after the flood, two women, local matriarchs, came to talk to me about how long this would all take. I was learning to tread gently but honestly. Maybe a little like an oncologist delivering bad news. I used phrases like 'it may take a while' and reassured them that some of us would stay to help long after the others have gone.

Floods are often a disaster planner's bread and butter. In some parts of the UK, their onslaught can be relent-less – spring, summer, autumn, early winter, late winter. Emergency planners learn how to plan for them, prevent them, respond to them, recover from them. Then do it all again.

Before 2007, they had always seemed just a little bit dull. 'Not bloody floods again,' colleagues would moan as they quickly scanned a newly released programme for that year's emergency planning national conference. Looking back, I was initially dismissive of the impact of flooding and did not consider it to be as 'dramatic' or 'traumatic' as the bomb explosions and air crashes I had worked on. There isn't a big DVI deployment. There are no glossy disaster management firms with an interest in the clean-up of floods. It is left to the local authority, the home-owner and the recalcitrant insurer. There are often no deaths, or only a small number – a farmer trapped trying to rescue livestock; the body of an older lady found in her bungalow only after the waters recede.

Wider public interest in a flood is similarly limited. On the day itself, local news reporters don boots and waders to report, breathlessly, from the thigh-deep water. They might return twice more. Once, two or three days later, for the 'everything in the sitting room is floating' piece, where they capture a sodden sofa and toys bobbing in the filthy broth. Ideally the home-owner will cry. Then again on the year's anniversary to show how the community is rebuilding, or sometimes to point out that the river is rising again. There is a terrible inevitability to flooding in the UK, particularly as our climate continues to change.

But in the end these floods truly schooled me, bashed me over the head with their carnage and their dismal, stinking power, and focused me in on the chronic aftermath of disaster. Flooding illustrates perfectly how in disaster, there are three waves of activity in my work. First of all there is the planning, which you hope will never need to see the light of day. But if the worst happens, what kicks in next is the immediate response and the short-term stabilisation. Finally, there comes the equally important much, much longer-term recovering. The bit that gets so little attention. There is a diagram that we use in training. It depicts the first response to an incident and shows two of the blue-light responders (fire and ambulance) as short, equal lines lingering for hours or a few days at most. The police investigation may take longer so their line edges a little further. But the longest line belongs to the local authority response. Coloured in orange, this line lingers on for years, to the edge of the diagram and almost off the page. It is entangled with the green line of a community that feels the loss for generations.

There is no external klaxon to mark the transition between these stages and imposing one artificially can feel clunky. In 2007, I was asked by the Cabinet Office to design a 'handover' certificate that police could sign and ceremoniously present to local authorities when response had transformed into recovery. But life after disaster is in reality a game of snakes and ladders. You can flood again, going right back to the response stage, while still recovering from the last one.

As planners, we teach each other to see 'Recovery' as a specific phase of the disaster and something that can be planned for in advance before the specifics of the emergency are known. To do this, planners are encouraged to write checklists, which include desired outcomes – such as schools being fully functional again or roads being rebuilt. The UK government definition of recovery also refers to a chance to seize the aftermath for 'regeneration' of an area – strengthening a disaster-stricken community by rebuilding more resilient homes or encouraging educational programmes. I am often heartened by those chances to build in little flashes of improvement – better flood defences, a new play park. All the while offering up a secret prayer to the gods that all the hard work will not be washed away a year later.

Those who have never been flooded assume that after a few weeks of drying out and a new lick of paint, a flood-damaged home will be habitable again. But that is rarely the case. The extent of the physical damage, and sometimes the financial complications too, can leave a family living, suspended, in temporary lodgings for eighteen or even twenty-four months. For most people, their home is situated within a network – other homes, shops, a park, 'a lifescape'[27] of important places and spaces. When the damage caused by a flood means a family or individual is moved to temporary accommodation elsewhere, they have usually lost everything or almost everything from their life before, and that includes the loss of a sense of home, of safety at home, of cosiness, as well as physical objects. This feeling can persist long after they return, back inside the supposedly familiar four walls. Even when a recovery is supposedly 'well established' and people were supposed to be healing, I have noticed that many residents stop using the word home at all.

In 2007, the residents of the council-managed housing in Toll Bar, asked – no, demanded – to be kept together rather than being dispersed to temporary accommodation across the county. To facilitate this, the council, many of whom lived locally themselves, created and managed a large park of fifty-two mobile homes and a laundry area built on a farmer's field. The rest of the residents moved in with relatives or into the upstairs of their house as it was 'remediated'.[28] This allowed residents to stay local, which went on to prove critical to the way in which people were able to maintain and rebuild their networks after the floods.

I made weekly trips to the village and was particularly keen to see the newly placed mobile homes procured by the council. The first time Tom drove me there, he low-whistled at the extent of destruction in the village. Boarded-up shops and washed-away front gardens. There was spray paint on one of the shop boards: 'We'll be back' and next to it, 'So will we'. Every single door to every single house was thrown open and the contents spewed out into the front lawn or into the recently arrived skips. Fans hummed and the red lights of hundreds of de-humidifiers made the scene look like an invasion of small aliens had taken place.

Survivors always underestimate how long it takes to dry everything out after even the smallest invasion of water. Flood damage to a home cleaves through the life before but, unlike fire, does not destroy it completely. It cruelly damages and contaminates just enough that the item is still there but is fouled. Personal possessions are either washed away or thrown into skips. If you have stored items upstairs, they may still become damaged by mould, or looted or destroyed before the building work starts. The residents in Toll Bar were told by the council that everything was contaminated with '*E coli* . . . from all the, you know, shit . . . the waste', so threw everything away – 'even Grandad's war medals' and 'all our birth certificates'. There was no expensive personal effects contract enacted here – no drying rooms or gift boxes. Later, I would be able to train local authorities to slow the recovery down a little, giving residents time to protect and dry out these treasures. Once, after I supported on the recovery after a flood in Wales, a Welsh Assembly member complained to the media that there was a mad academic trying to persuade people to fish about in the sewage.

The caravan park the Doncaster responders had built to house the displaced was adjacent to the majority of damaged homes and opposite the primary school. The tearing apart of the homes would last for almost a year. The residents had to trust they would be built back up again. The downstairs were scoured and sandblasted back to bare plaster but on the upstairs bedroom windowsill you could still see lots and lots of teddies, thick with dust and dirt.

Disaster survivors face a steady chain of losses and one of the first is a loss of privacy. The caravans were close to each other and right on the road. I could see right into their lives. 'It's one, great big goldfish bowl,' said a member of staff.

One caravan had a tent attached to it which was set up like a living room and was completely open to the elements. Every time I went back it attracted my attention because it changed with the seasons: a pumpkin for Halloween in autumn, decorated for Christmas in December. The constant signs of an ongoing battle to keep going – eating, playing and doing homework.

Some of the families had no insurance at all, as is commonly found after UK disasters. It is estimated that up to 20 per cent of households are without insurance across the UK, with figures higher in many areas. Many more households have policies that leave them underinsured, and for some faiths insurance is forbidden. Those with insurance were told by their companies that they would be committing fraud if they tried to keep anything because they were being compensated for the losses. So everything had to go into the skip. To make sure, the insurance companies sent contractors to the older people's bungalows to cut up their family's furniture in front of them. For the families with no insurance, the council danced a delicate ballet in the background, hooking them up with charities and the church. I visited one family who had received a donation of a fridge and a microwave, but no carpets. They moved around on newspapers and sat on plastic garden chairs left by the builders.

I talked to the residents and listened to their regrets for hours. The talk often turned to what they missed most and could replace. The residents jokingly referred to me as 'the Skip Lady' because I had taken such interest in what they had been told to throw away. The skips had been there for weeks, cloaked in the smell of rot. There was rubble and food, but there were also so many personal belongings. Christmas decorations, shoes, lots of children's toys, cheque-books and a hundred photographs.

Photographs were the most frequently mentioned loss by all residents. When I first visited the scene, there were still four-by-six glossy individual photographs floating in the puddles. For the younger women, the most common loss was their pregnancy ultrasound photos. Doncaster Royal Infirmary charged five pound coins for one single photo. You put the coins in and get a token and give that to the midwife. There is also a warning sign next to the machine that they should not be photocopied, though the reasons for this are vague. In these days before ubiquitous camera phones, many only had one photograph.

The next time I met the residents, I found that two of the older women had downloaded some of my newly written national guidance on the return of personal effects. They had caught a bus to the town library and brought back books on climate change and my documents wrapped in plastic supermarket bags. They interrogated me roughly as to why their items did not get the same attention as I had recommended for the belongings of those affected by a bomb attack and I had no answers. I took my findings back to the Cabinet Office and arranged an urgent seminar with the Association of British Insurers but the same thing happened for the next ten years. Floods are just seen as *different*. Not as devastating.

The things we own make up what the sociologist Kai Erikson calls the 'furniture of self'.[29] They are part of what makes us *us* and their loss can be felt as keenly as that of people or places. I would return home from these visits to my things, to my clutter, feeling intensely guilty about having a sofa and a bath. Even a place to set up an ironing board. The residents missed all of these things and talked about them often.

I was a regular fixture in the village by the second year and many of the residents asked me to come and see their remediated houses. Finally they were back in and the builders and plumbers and electricians had left. They had reclaimed their front gardens, filling them with flower tubs or children's toys or recycling and wheelie bins. This reclamation, through brightly coloured plastic tubs and spinning plastic flowers, is something I have seen all around the world. The neighbourhood centre had now gone; the caravan park was just a field again. But their shadowy memory remained. There were holes where they had been – a mark and a space. And the tidemark of the flood water was an indelible patina. 'The water marks are our scars,' said several residents.

I had met Karen at the early meetings in the leisure centre two summers before. Now she showed me into a very full house, every surface covered almost as if she was reclaiming every last bit of the house from the water. The sitting room was full of toys and there was a computer, TV, sofa and, over the fireplace, a big new picture of Karen's three children. Two dogs had the run of the kitchen and their bowls and beds were strewn across it. I asked what she felt was missing in her house since the floods. She turned the question round because there was actually only one thing here from before: 'the fruit elephant'. This was a little ceramic elephant holding a fruit bowl and was all that remained of what had been a much bigger set. She had bought some other little ceramic elephants in a charity shop a few weeks ago to join him but it wasn't the same. They had none of the stories that had gone with the ones before.

Karen and the other residents lived in fear of the floods coming again. We were joined by Pam, who had become a flood warden for the local council, partly so that she would feel informed. 'You need to be involved to get the information,' she said conspiratorially and deadly serious. They had arrangements with friends to let each other know as soon as they heard anything. People got very worried in downpours and they were worried in January again when the rugby field flooded. Some of the children at the school would soil themselves when they realised it was raining.

The residents were organising their annual carnival. There was a bucking bronco ordered and plans for a competition for a 'gala queen'. They wanted to do something hopeful for the children. These felt like shoots of recovery. Some of the residents had also been pleased to be invited to a government workshop with the Cabinet Office National Recovery Team in London and were looking forward to sharing their experiences, but then nothing had come of it. 'We never went. They never sent us any details, no confirmation . . . nothing.' People were very angry; some had taken holiday from work to go. They felt like an afterthought.

They were not emotional people, they said, but the tears were there, 'under the surface', all the time. 'I am definitely showing emotion more,' said Karen. When we stepped outside, Pam's garden gate, two doors down, was open – the yard was immaculate with flowers and a lush lawn and her husband was working in one of three small sheds. Pam's black Labrador, who swam out of that gate two years ago and then travelled with them to the leisure centre, brought me a toy and shoved it into my leg. Pam pointed out where the grass had died and then grown back differently after the water. It didn't die immediately but died in patches some time later. 'Do you know what the council man said to me?' she said. 'The grass was *stressed* after the floods.' She laughed, hard, at the irony.

I went back and forth to Toll Bar for over a decade, during which I also found myself being called to other communities all around the country, who were back at day one, watching people hang their wet clothes over radiators in leisure centres. I never talked of recovering as linear again, now understanding how easy it is to set a community back in their efforts. I also understood why so many activists rally against the term 'natural disasters' – because while the causes of the event – the flood or the quake – may be rooted in geography, they are compounded by both human error and human frailty. It wouldn't be long before I saw this in action again, on the other side of the world.

Every two years, an international conference on disaster reconstruction and recovery would be held for global 'recoverers' and in 2008, I was asked to present two papers in Christchurch, New Zealand. I presented about the attempts by Doncaster council to protect the 'lifescapes' of the local people and also my own campaigning to protect their personal effects. I was utterly captivated by the country. New Zealand had a feeling of how the UK could be if we had just been nicer to each other. I particularly enjoyed my time in Christchurch. Eating a ginormous ice cream cone in the square outside the cathedral, I sat back on my chair and thought there was nowhere more beautiful on earth. Four years later, I was invited back to speak again. But by now, the cathedral was a wreck and the epicentre of a raging, destructive debate about how and when to rebuild.

At 4.35 a.m. on 4 September 2010, an earthquake measuring 7.1 on the Richter scale had struck the Canterbury region of New Zealand. It was centred

11km beneath the rural town of Darfield, 40km away. There was extensive damage to buildings and infrastructure but no deaths. Canterbury residents breathed a sigh of relief: things could have been so much worse. But then, more than five months after the main shock, on 22 February 2011, an aftershock of 6.3 on the Richter scale occurred 5km south-east of Christchurch at a depth of only 5km. This time, the earthquake struck at lunchtime on a working day, causing catastrophic damage to the city and resulting in 185 deaths.

When I visited a year later, the ground was still shaking. My host, Brenda, a researcher at Massey University, a responder and a resident, whose own home and workplace had been severely damaged, took me to a high point outside of Christchurch so that I could look down on the scale of the destruction. It was biblical. One thing I had never fully appreciated before was the damage done by something called 'liquefaction' in the aftermath of an earthquake. The liquid mud that bubbles up from below the earth's surface was almost as destructive as the effects of the earthquake itself. Over 900,000 tonnes of the thick, grey silt had to be removed from just the city itself. It had also caused long-term contamination to the water supply and structural damage.

But it was when we drove as close as we could to the 'red zone' at the heart of the state that what had been lost really hit me. Thousands and thousands of homes, schools, shops, churches and temples had been declared too unsafe to return to after a number of rapid geological assessments. Some were damaged, some were not, but they simply could not be lived in any more. Brenda pointed out where people would sneak in through gaps in the metal fencing to mow their front lawn.

Brenda took me to her own home to see the huge cracks in the walls and the Christchurch 'lean' – every shelf now at an angle as the building subsided. She also showed me her composting toilet; residents had been advised to build these if they had the means to do so due to the damage to the state's sewerage systems. Brenda's was in a shed and had a proper seat over a long drop. Fairy lights were strung over it and friends and family would write messages of hope on the walls: a show of defiance and resilience even in the loo.

Just as with Toll Bar, my time in Christchurch showed me again the complicated network of physical structures and human behaviours that entwine to make up a place. By now, I had attended so many incidents and training exercises where the scenario would be thrown in like a tennis ball and it would simply be batted back with a neat solution. 'We need to evacuate residents from a nursing home.' Thwack, the ball is returned. 'No problem, we have spaces in twenty other homes. Put them in those alphabetically.' Job done. But a well-run, safe nursing home is a community of its own. We had just ripped that apart – not the earthquake, *us*, the responders. We could have sat with our decision for ten minutes, worked it through. In the heat of response, it can be hard to sell the idea that a bit more time and trouble is worth it. That valuing the meaning of those connections and then finding ways to protect them would make our lives easier in the recovery, too. Often the solution is relatively simple. An extra afternoon spent with residents or their carers working out over a cup of tea whether some groups could be kept together. In Christchurch, 250 residents of nursing homes were 'redistributed' to homes outside the state.

The New Zealanders had sought support and personnel from UK DVI (Disaster Victim Identification) and I had provided technical advice to the team that was deployed following the huge February aftershock. There had been a major Disaster Victim Identification operation in the affected areas as most of the deceased had been burnt in fires that occurred after the buildings collapsed. By the time their flights had landed, the New Zealand media had already condemned police and local authorities for being too slow with the identification.

It became clear to me that the authorities were greatly struggling in their communications with bereaved families. They had made a mistake I had seen so many times before. Police who had told families that their loved ones had died instantly were then caught out by CCTV played at inquest showing the person waving for help from a window. This well-intentioned dishonesty strips away the trust between responder and the bereaved and sets them back. 'If that was a lie, what else is untrue,' they wonder and tumble back to the raw, aching maw of the first hours of waiting for news.

*   *   *

One of the most painful similarities that I have encountered in the aftermath of disasters is that almost everyone, including the community and responders, is in denial about how long this will hurt for. They want to believe that life after disaster is a fleeting state. They stay stuck in a bargaining/denial phase of a grief cycle, lashing out at organisations around them for failing to take the pain away.

One of the first, urgent questions that the Christchurch-based 'recoverers' had for me was, 'What next?' They assumed that once remediation of the thousands of damaged spaces had occurred, there would be a chance to move on. And that the honeymoon of initial collaboration – cheering of the fire trucks, fairy lights strung up in loos and a 'student army' of young people who cleared the liquefaction from the streets – would last. They had thought people would blame the earth's tectonic plates, not building control or search and rescue services. They had not planned for a legal aftermath and forensic uncertainty. There was genuine bewilderment among responders that things seemed to be getting worse, not better. 'But how long does it feel like this?' they would ask over and over.

But disasters are about total loss. Tangible losses: of a person, a house, a place. And intangible losses: of a feeling of safety, trust in authority. And then the terrible mourning for the life before. The best way to describe it is a word originating in Wales: *hiraeth*. The first time I heard the word was from those speaking and writing about the tragedy at the Welsh village of Aberfan, a terrible disaster that killed 144 people. In

October 1966, a colliery spoil tip crashed onto the school and houses below. One hundred and sixteen of the dead were children. *Hiraeth* is a longing for a place to which there is no return, an echo of something that can never be found, a heartsickness for something that no longer exists and a time that can never be gone back to.

At one talk, I played a video of the Hillsborough anniversary service from April 2009, the twentieth anniversary of the disaster, held, as it always is, annually, at the Liverpool Football Club stadium. As a government minister is speaking he is suddenly drowned out by a whole stadium of community members chanting 'Justice for the 96'. He bows his head, clearly overcome with emotion.[30] For those in the stadium, their pain, bewilderment and anger is still as real as it was 240 months earlier.

The New Zealanders crowded round me in the coffee break afterwards. Surely there was some mistake. Surely this was specific to Hillsborough. This could not go on for twenty years.

There is some debate about whether the disaster is the initial 'big bang' or the years that follow. After Toll Bar and Christchurch, it was clear to me that life after disaster is perpetual, chronic, with a pain that ebbs and flows like tides. And that errors made in the response can change the course of the recovery and undermine the longer-term psycho-social health of whole communities.

Before the floods, I thought I knew what trauma was and what causes it. But in the floodwaters of

Doncaster and the rubble of Christchurch, I discovered a new, long, chronic loss brought about by the loss of everything. The 'furniture of self' laid to waste. The never-ending ache of *hiraeth*. But these places also taught me something else. The value of a horizon to swim towards. The importance of trying to build something afterwards. But to stay living, breathing, there had to be a purpose, a future, a bluer sky.

7

Little Losses

Tom and I were married in New York in November 2007. We eloped (neither of us wanted a fuss) and the actor Alan Ruck, from our favourite film *Ferris Bueller's Day Off* was our witness. Sometimes the stars align in a good way, too. He was ahead of us in the queue waiting for his own marriage licence and the convention is that those ahead in the queue perform the duty for a couple without witnesses. My new husband and I had lunch in a café and then emailed our families from the public library.

Tom was, by then, the captain of a commercial 737 jet. He knew that I kept strange company but, as I also had an academic position, he tended to describe me to colleagues as a scholar and a planner, without much mention of the disaster part. It would have soured the mood in the cockpit to have entered into discussion with his first officer about what I actually did – and by then he wasn't completely sure. I knew that it was very important that my work never came home. Even with all the technical and engineering know-how in the world and the certainty of safe systems, it takes an amount of blind faith to sit in command in the cockpit of an aircraft, straddling tens of tons of kerosene. For him to be able to do that every day he needed to be able to train for an almost-worst-case scenario but one that he could always control. A bird strike or an engine failure is routinely tested in the simulator and he trained to handle it. Climbing into our bed every night, I was a grotesque reminder of his very worst-case scenario. The time that he might not be able to steer himself out of trouble. One night, he came to pick me up from the train station after a visit to the scene of a crash. There had been no chance for a shower. 'Why do you smell of aviation fuel?' he asked and then wished he hadn't.

We drove home in silence.

The first time Tom and I lost a baby, I kept the pregnancy test, scan photos and the first midwife's appointment card in a box. There was a comfort in that but, more importantly to me, it was the proof that she had *been*. She had existed. By the time I came to fill my own box, I had spent five years working on the design and durability of 'memory boxes' with police forces and mortuary teams all around the world. Containers in which to give families those few items that were left a charred passport, a printout of their phone data, a gold signet ring, the wrapper from a packet of mints.

The type and the construction of the box was crucial. Too 'gifty' and it looked all wrong; too flimsy and the bottom might fall out just at the moment we handed it over to the family. The Metropolitan police went through an unfortunate phase of wrapping items in recycled paper that had been pulped with wild flowers. The 'artisan' result was quietly scrapped when families complained that they had been shocked by the flecked paper, thinking that the little imperfections were bits of blood or ash. I picked a brightly coloured shoebox as my first memory box.

I always knew when my babies had died, at least three or four days before it was confirmed by an ultrasound scan or the commencement of a clotty haemorrhage. I would wake up, place my hand on my belly and, like so many before me, I would simply *know*. Women's voices are constantly marginalised in their own medicine and their own care, and so what would often follow over the next few days was a series of condescending exchanges about how 'all mummies worry'. Due to a clotting disease, diagnosed after the third loss, my miscarriages would generally occur not long after my twelve-week scan. So I had already seen a living foetus and a heartbeat when the placenta stopped working. Once they had seen that heartbeat, the midwives would reassure me that it would be fine. *This* baby would be fine. This time. Their words would influence Tom, who was trained by his profession to listen to and respect a hierarchy of knowledge and experience. He would make crisis tea and head off to work for a long night flight, reassured by a clinician's voice.

But I would sit in the dark and say goodbye. And then I would call Jay, my taxi driver, but more of a big, tattooed brother by now. 'Hospital?' was all he would need to ask after the first couple of trips. Several times he had to stop the car for me to throw up on a verge, the last of the pregnancy hormones still playing a cruel trick. He would take me to the early pregnancy unit, the same one he had visited with his wife several times, and ask that I text him with an update.

'It'll be reet, Luce,' he would say as I clambered out of the car. He didn't mean today; we both knew today would not be reet. It would be shitty. He meant, eventually, in the longer term, it would be OK. Jay would have been a great recovery planner. He is as certain in his own belief system as any priest or reverend that I have ever met that in the end it will work out.

After I had bled so badly with the first one, some of the others were cleared out of me with an operation to 'evacuate the retained products of conception' or 'ERPC'. How I came to hate that term and the way that the acronym tripped of the nurses' and doctors' tongues. No different from the way that we overuse RVP or SCG or SAGE in the world of UK disaster response,[31] using our acronyms to exclude and to mark out our tribal boundaries.

The procedure would be done, I would wake from a general anaesthetic and I would join six or seven other women in a sweaty gynaecology ward. The strange and overly-intimate camaraderie that formed there reminded me of the mortuary, full of conversations that could have no handle or meaning outside this space. I helped a woman calculate the likely weight loss at her Slimming World class now that her ovaries and her womb had been removed. One time I awoke to the hospital chaplain holding my hand, tears running down her face, whispering prayers into my ear. There had been some confusion and she was crying over the wrong patient. I was not the person who had asked for her and I had not lost a baby at thirty-eight weeks. Embarrassed, she hurried away, but I kept her prayers for myself.

There was no privacy granted or expected and the woman in the next bed would often offer a view on what the consultant had just said to me. If I was placed next to older women, they would offer comfort from their own stories. 'Don't worry love, it will be your turn next. We've all been there. I've got three girls now, and they have all had girls . . .' I was lucky that I could at least make the babies, I was told, IVF being as expensive as it is. Now all they needed to do was find a way for my poor old failing carcass to hold on to them.

Tom would collect me, having laid old towels across the car seat. 'Oooh a pilot,' the older women would coo as I gathered up my handbags and my blood-stained pyjamas. 'Lovely.'

Tom tenderly named the first one Titan, after the Greek gods, hoping that the name would imbue his tiny heir with the strength to survive. And they were always Titan after that. When you deliver a lost foetus at home, the process can take a number of forms. Sometimes you can deliver a tiny little baked-bean baby inside a fluid bubble. Other times, she exits in pieces. My first Titan took the latter approach. Easily identifiable parts leaked out of me over the course of a month. Her arm, a few centimetres long, reminded me of the tiny bones that they had tried so hard to name in New York. But she had no bones to keep or inter, she had not formed those yet. She had no burial site but to flush her away seemed a violation. The advice from the hospital had been vague. The first time, I collected what I could and took it with me to the midwife; she looked horrified and hurried them into a clinical waste bin. On another visit, the main parts of my twenty-eight-gram child were fished out with tweezers by a male medical student and placed into a kidney dish, just like the ones that had collected the bullets in our mortuaries.

Tom, watching horrified by the bed, was given a crumpled form and a pen and asked to tick if he wanted a funeral. He didn't. He wanted a baby. And a wife who wasn't utterly broken inside. This was the first time Tom had ever seen that form. But I knew it well. I had been part of its development.

Back before my career in disaster had properly started, immediately after my graduation from Bristol in the summer of 2000, I had taken a placement with the new coroner for the busy and demanding office of Liverpool. As I arrived, the staff were under siege, dealing with a monumental scandal. The coroner's pathologist had been storing human remains for over a decade without the knowledge or consent of the families – a practice which, it emerged, was also occurring all around the country. The scandal had emerged as evidence in another inquiry somewhere else. When giving evidence into the high number of children's deaths during heart surgery at Bristol Royal Infirmary, a witness made it clear that there were repositories of children's organs being held indefinitely. The largest of these collections was at the Alder Hey Children's Hospital in Liverpool and this repository would give its name to the whole scandal.

An investigation was started and it became clear that one particular pathologist at Alder Hey, Professor van Velzen, had gone far beyond any medical school conventions at the time. Rather than keeping a carefully curated collection of tissue, recovered with consent, he had become bogged down in an administrative backlog. It also appeared that he had deliberately kept all sorts of material for research projects that he had never completed. He had kept every single organ of some patients, returning only a hollowed husk to their loved ones without relatives' knowledge. He had kept the bodies of new babies and unborn babies too tiny to survive in a hidden practice that had lasted for years. Other hospitals, coroners' offices and police stores realised that they too held a similar repository, albeit on a smaller scale. I watched as coronial teams all around the country swapped notes on how to return the fragments of long-dead loved ones that had been retained by their own pathology teams. Blocks of brain tissue, smears of blood on slides.

Van Velzen's research had a particular focus on the development of babies and foetuses and whether the failure of development in their organs predisposed them to sudden infant death syndrome. The later inquiry showed that as he became overwhelmed with his work and neglected his practice, the tiniest of our society kept coming to his labs but he did no research on them. He simply stored them. The Liverpool coroner and his team, many with their own infants at home, were trying to respond to a hidden crisis with a casualty list of thousands. Little casualties who had never even been born, traceable only through their mothers' details.

Since then, I have met a number of families who received a letter or a phone call asking them to make contact with their local coroner or the team in place to reunite families with pieces of their family member – pieces they had not known were even missing. Mothers who were told in the 1980s that it was hospital policy to take away their twenty-two-week foetus.

When giving evidence to the later public inquiry, a common theme among parents was that they had been given no further information after the bodies were taken away. Some thought that they were donating their child's organs for transplantation to other children. Other parents of older children found out that all they actually buried was some skin and tissue while the majority of their child was still in a lab. Not at rest.

I learned a lot in those summer weeks about the attachment, the weight that we put on to the fragments of our loved ones. Then I learned it all over again when those tiny parts were from within.

So the form that they handed Tom wasn't new to me. The UK had passed strict tissue management laws in the wake of the scandal and I had later been involved in several government workshops about the development of the paperwork to accompany it. Like all government-designed tools, it was tested and tweaked and focus-grouped. I had even turned it into worksheets for my own teaching on tissue consent.

As Tom ticked a box handing the tiny parts over to the hospital for a joint cremation with lots of other loss, I turned to the wall so that the two men in the room wouldn't see me cry.

Still bleeding, I headed back into the fray, attending exercises and giving talks wearing big pants and maxi pads. I tried to bury myself in writing scenarios and planning. Only my mum and a few close friends would comment on how pale I was looking, glancing nervously at my still-rounded belly which would no longer justify a seat on the London Underground. The men of the Emergency Planning College showed their solidarity through a squeeze of an arm or by making me a cup of tea when their training course broke for refreshments five minutes earlier, placing an extra custard cream on the saucer.

Tom and I grieved separately, with neither wanting to upset the other. Instead, I found solace in strange, quiet places. The mortuary, the laboratories, the back of a coroner's court. My work brought me into regular contact with Lucina Hackman, one of the country's leading anthropologists. We had first started sharing conference stages in the early 2000s. Anthros often seem to be built differently from the other scientists in the mortuary. They care as much about their anthropology as their forensic science – about the person before them and about the rites that need to be applied to the bones. The forensic anthropologists are a very special tribe to me. It is a vocation that attracts more women scientists than any other branch of forensic medicine and has been revolutionised, stewarded, governed and protected by a fearsome band of matriarchs – in this country, Baroness Professor Dame Sue Black at their forefront.

I looked forward to my regular trips to Lucina's university in Dundee, which was the centre for much of the UK DVI training and world-renowned for its work in forensic science. They ran scene management and body recovery and also the only course in the country that allowed DVI police officers to work with actual deceased in training.

As befits someone who spends a large amount of time with the dead and their skeletons, asking them for answers, Lucina has an uncanny ability to know what you are thinking and what you need before you articulate it. One of my visits to her laboratories had coincided with yet another bloody loss. This one had come later in the pregnancy and the foetus, another little girl, had been sent for post-mortem. We had ticked the box for the baby to be cremated with the other losses that month and be scattered in the hospital bereavement garden. A letter had arrived, in amongst local leaflets about recycling and other unremarkable mail, that told us it had been done. I handed it to Tom without words and he shook his head sadly, placed it on top of the bread bin and went to make a cup of tea. Another one gone. I put the letter in her memory box.

Lucina is curator for one of the most complete collections of pre-natal bones in the world. The collection is fiercely guarded to limit access and there is no destructive research – any research that would involve damage – allowed. After we had finished our meeting and eaten lasagne in the university canteen, we sat in the space where the collection is housed. We talked about work and husbands and the care required to keep a colony of dermestid beetles healthy. Lucina is incredibly protective of her beetles. She uses them to strip flesh from the animal bones she uses as teaching aids as it's less destructive than any chemical or surgical methods. But the beetles can be temperamental, she told me, and were developing a taste for pheasant and rejecting other meats.

The whole time we talked, Lucina was wearing magician's white cloth gloves, preparing a tiny infant skull for scanning. I peered in closer, expecting it to appear as fragile as a bird's skull in a hedgerow, and was surprised to see that it was much stronger looking than that. It was distinctively a person's skull, not a bird or animal. I studied it for an eternity. This child had developed almost to term, whereas my latest had never got to grow its complement of forty-four skull bone structures. But the sense of what could have been felt the same.

Lucina said nothing but she knew that I was saying goodbye.

8

The Fear

'Lucy, I don't know ... this looks like a big one ...'
Nick, the national lead for the UK Disaster Victim
Identification unit, panted down the phone, partly
from the severity of the situation but also from the
exertion of a walk across Whitehall. He was rushing to
the Cabinet Office briefing rooms, a group of meeting rooms in 70 Whitehall in London used to co-
ordinate the different parts of government at the time
of a crisis. 'Lucy, they're saying this one could be ...
as big as Chernobyl.'

Nick sounded afraid. I have seen real fear in the faces
of the disaster response community and heard it in
their voices only a few times. Normally, I see a pumped-
up, charged, *up for it* set to the jaw. Particularly when
the situation is terrorist related. *Bring it on*, the angry
eyes of the responders seem to say. But in the days and
nights following the Fukushima disaster in March 2011
I remember witnessing the purest fear.

Few people outside the disaster planning world
realise how close the world came to complete catastrophe in early 2011. At the time, among other things,

I was working on a contract at Sellafield, in Cumbria, one of the world's oldest and largest nuclear facilities, to review its emergency management arrangements and specifically those in the event of a 'mass fatality'. It had been a discomfiting insight into the wafer-thin lines between safety and total annihilation. The Sellafield plant was going through a number of massive infrastructure programmes. The nuclear waste we have created globally will outlive us all, stored in its rusting pools of toxic water. In a society with nuclear power, the risk of nuclear meltdown is always present and in the back of all planners' minds is the Chernobyl disaster in 1986. Over time, the accident at the Chernobyl plant in northern Ukraine is believed to have killed thousands of people and injured by radiation contamination millions more. It is estimated that the land around the site will be uninhabitable for 20,000 years.[32]

I really thought another Chernobyl had come to pass that spring. On 11 March, the most powerful earthquake ever recorded in Japan and the fourth biggest ever recorded in the world unleashed a tsunami onto the east of the country. Waves reaching 40 metres raced inland and disabled the power supply and therefore the cooling of three Fukushima Daiichi reactors. All three cores largely melted in the first three days, and the technical picture suggested this was much worse than anything seen in nuclear accidents before. The initial scientific information was dire but there seemed to be relative calm among the UK public and in the media. They did not seem to pick up on the terrors being conveyed to the government about the impending catastrophe.

We were responding to two disasters simultaneously. It was clear that thousands of people had died in the tsunami but we also did not yet know what role the nuclear emergency would play. Of a death toll of just under 20,000 killed by the waves, the initial, unconfirmed, figures were suggesting that over 900 Britons were dead.

'War rooms' are established in Cabinet Office meeting rooms to allow ministers from all government departments to meet for the most serious incidents. They are chaired by the prime minister or a government minister from the department most closely aligned to the incident. The group has become known as COBR – Cabinet Office briefing room, with an 'A' tacked on.[33] 'COBRA' sounds cool, like the snake, and perpetuates an idea that James Bond and his scientists are at the helm. COBR is the start of the fantasy of control. I have been deep to the hallowed halls in the belly of Whitehall a few times for disaster planning meetings. When I first went, they asked us politely to not take any photos on our phone; now they take them off you at the door. I wonder if it is so you can't show the world how shabby it is, how 'normal'.

At times of disaster, central government is also advised by a core group of scientists. This is known as the Scientific Advisory Group on Emergencies (SAGE). Only certain types of science make the cut. It is very focused on the immediacy of the disaster and on highly technical, number-heavy reports. SAGE often has no appetite for the long-term consequences of disaster and their implications on a slow and painful recovery.

But Nick was leading on the implications for a DVI response to Japan and wanted me involved. I was given the title of 'Tactical Adviser' to UK DVI and Nick fed my reports straight into COBR. An unequal, uncomfortable coalition government between David Cameron's Conservative party and Nick Clegg's Liberal Democrats had recently been formed and the new ministers were unseasoned in disaster response. The mood in March 2011 was made worse by an update from the mammoth technology company Google, who was trialling a new crisis response website that would find and reunite people in a crisis. Their numbers looked bleak.

I was set to work on a UK body recovery, repatriation and family assistance plan. This looked like a highly complex disaster and the circumstances were grim. And this was before we factored in the threat of nuclear annihilation. The deceased had been killed by the tsunami but the second, pending disaster could make them unreachable. I knew by then that families who have a body learn to grieve. When there is no body they can only simply exist. The Japanese normally have a series of complicated rites and rituals in death but 20,000 dead on one day would quickly overwhelm. And when there is a lot of death at one time, surviving communities can become so fearful of the dead, worried that they will spread disease, that they forego usual rites. Remains are hastily tipped into mass graves or cremated, and lost forever. Most of my conversations about bringing our dead home from Japan were conducted by phone or Skype for the simple reason that our newborn baby daughter, the first to grow to term, was only a few days old. Elizabeth arrived one month early and, having waited so long for her, it seemed bloody ironic that she had burst into the world at a point when it seemed to be in the grip of nuclear disaster. I could not allow myself to believe that she would make it, so had set about completing my PhD while I waited for the inevitable loss to happen. We had even agreed that Tom would take a six-month secondment to Québec City, allowing him to experience flying around the US and the Caribbean. I would join him if, and when, my pregnancy was lost again. But I never did get to visit him. A combination of heparin injections and steroids, to thin my blood and suppress my immune system, meant that at each scan she was still there.

Her arrival was an emergency and Tom was still overseas in Québec. I was alone for the birth, and for the emergency C-section and the blood transfusions that followed. When he arrived to meet her, in the same clothes in which he had boarded the first of four flights, three days earlier, the women on the ward and the midwives clapped and cheered. We brought her home from the hospital and struggled to believe she was finally here, smiling at each other drunk with tiredness over the top of her perfect head.

While Elizabeth slept, I contacted colleagues all around Asia with eyes on the ground and eventually was able to talk to somebody directly who worked in death planning in Sendai, near to where the earthquake had struck. The situation was so dire, they said, they would have to revisit plans only previously seen at Hiroshima and Nagasaki. They would be using mass graves and there would be no way that a UK DVI team could be hosted. I informed COBR that we may have a serious problem. It could be impossible to recover these bodies.

My career has coincided with a massive escalation of awareness around 'contaminating' threats and accidents – nuclear, chemical, weaponised biological and radiological. When I first started work at Kenyon, they were just taking stock of what these risks would mean to their business. They had encountered contaminants before, having operated during the Cold War and in the aftermath of Chernobyl. More recently, during the invasion of Iraq, depleted uranium was a muted concern in Brize Norton, and we had tried to ready ourselves for what might happen if Saddam Hussein used any of the 'weapons of mass destruction'. We also knew that contamination can be accidental too: jet airliners are made up of hundreds of thousands of dangerous constituents, and sometimes in the cargo too, so you could never assume that there were not chemical or radiological hazards following a crash and it was in all our aviation response plans.

The first time I encountered just how much brico-lage, how many complex odd jobs carried out by emergency responders behind the scenes, go into a CBRNE (chemical, biological, radiological and nuclear)[34] response was in the aftermath of the poison-ing of Alexander Litvinenko in November 2006. It is believed that polonium, the rare and highly radioac-tive metal that killed the former KGB agent, was placed into his cup of tea at a central London venue. What is less well known is that the perpetrator had also contaminated multiple venues by wandering around with this potentially fatal radioactive source. Every single point of contamination had to be tracked down using dosimetry, where small hand-held devices are used to measure radiation. I was advising the Home Office on disaster planning at the time and we received regular updates on the work being under-taken by ordinary people at Westminster City Council. It was a trail of deadly mess: hotel bedrooms and bathrooms, laundry chutes, planes, football clubs and lap dancing bars. Testing was undertaken in over fifty locations and more than a hundred people required follow up from health agencies. To reduce the harm of a gamma agent like polonium you only need to permanently fix a wooden board, or even something as thin as paper, over the contaminated area. But you have to find the radiation first.

The scale of the mess was not entirely a surprise: several branches of the Russian intelligence services are specifically trained not just to target their intended victim but also to leave a clear message via a trail of destruction-in-perpetuity around them. There is a long history of the use of radioactive and chemical agents to settle scores in this way and it was not the first time it had happened on UK soil. Nor would it be the last – most recently, in the towns of Salisbury and Amesbury, a Novichok nerve agent caused havoc across shopping centres, an air ambulance base, police headquarters, pubs and a housing complex used by vulnerable adults fighting addiction. The main target was a Russian agent and his daughter but the methods deployed by state terrorists were intended to be dramatic and far-reaching. Those transporting the radioactive or chemical poison often appear to make little attempt to control their terrifying cargo, meaning its legacy is sprayed liberally.

After the Litvinenko incident, public and media interest moved on, but the remediation took months and there are still teams watching over it today. With incidents involving contamination, the differences between response and recovery become even more acute. The response is more urgent than ever and involves speed, shouting and lots and lots of kit. Recovery, on the other hand, is underpinned by a dark and malignant fear that colours every aspect of the process.

The CBRNE world is the most macho and militaristic of all our fields. Every month, a magazine arrives at my house advertising the latest CBRNE kit – body bags that can contain anthrax within their seams, hand-held devices to detect toxic gases and sealed hoods that offer the 'ultimate in respiratory protection'. There is a great deal of fear involved in CBRNE.

The chemicals and substances are invisible and undeniably terrifying and I find this can distract responders from humanitarian needs. I have lectured at many CBRNE training events, often as one of only two or three women in a hundred, and there is always an assumption that because some of the risks we discuss are so deadly, all normal rites and rituals, protections and sensibilities must be stripped away. Muslim women must be ordered to undress in the town centre, older people sealed into their nursing homes, pets will need to be shot and personal effects burned on pyres. People will comply or die.

It is true that in CBRNE incidents, government agencies must be very firm, even aggressive, towards the public just to get control of the situation. They are forced to use a lot of command and control statements. Normal interactions are stripped away and medical personnel may need to become faceless humanoids in masks, increasing feelings of panic. Distance is imperative in a CBRNE incident but if we are not careful we remove all that makes us human and then it is very hard in the recovery phase to pull the public back into trusting us.

Many emergency planners shy away from CBRNE completely. The scenarios are the hardest of all to plan for because there is no end point. The response phase is finite, maybe hours, days or months, but it will creak to an ending eventually. Whereas the recovery phase, the 'afterwards', both physical and psychological, can be infinite. Chernobyl will always be Chernobyl. For all of the incidents I have ever been involved in where contamination is a concern, I have urged the responders to dial down their use of fear of long-term contamination and simply deal with the issues calmly, while explaining to the communities what the science says. However serious the harm, people have to have hope for the future. I also campaign for planners to think about whether their verbal messages of reassurance – i.e., that the risk was low and managed – were contradicted by how they were behaving on the ground. Because the fear spreads.

I think back to how flooded residents in Toll Bar and across the country were whipped into a frenzy about contamination due to the barrage of media messaging regarding floodwater and a risk of *E coli*, in many cases leading to them throwing away possessions they could have saved out of fear that they could make them sick. In certain government corridors there was a feeling that the public were overreacting. These agencies felt that their messaging and information was clear and balanced and they did not understand why the public was alarmed. What they didn't consider was that when these agencies came to clean up, they arrived in unmarked vans, in Tyvek white suits and masks with disinfecting sprayers, refused to speak to the public and created an atmosphere of fear and uncertainty.

In my efforts I have found allies in this along the way in many unusual places. The scientists of the Defence Science and Technical Laboratories at Porton Down have always welcomed my pleas to protect the personal effects and the care of the relatives, finding ways to decontaminate wedding rings exposed to Novichok and polonium. My visits to them always take me back to an early visit to a midwife who asked me if I was avoiding soft, unpasteurised cheeses. I nodded meekly and did not inform her that while I was avoiding brie like the plague, just the day before I had been on a tour of laboratories safely housing the 21 most dangerous pathogens in the world.

The initial horror we feared from those early briefings didn't come to pass. On paper the damage to the reactors looked far worse than anything ever seen before. But over a number of days it became clear that Armageddon had been averted. The nuclear disaster was declared to be a level 7 incident, the only one to reach this level apart from Chernobyl, but there were some key differences between the two. In Japan much of the radiation was discharged into the Pacific Ocean and there was international praise for the clean-up efforts. However, many areas of Fukushima continue to be uninhabitable. What to do with the reactor continues to be contentious.

The terrible effects of the earthquake and tsunami got a little lost in the nuclear noise but this other disaster devastated parts of Japan. Some 20,000 people lost their lives in the tsunami and earthquake, with a further 2,500 still missing. Many of the bodies were left in the open air for weeks and, although cremation is a key part of Japanese death rituals, the authorities were forced to resort to using mass graves. The majority of the bodies had to be identified by visual methods alone (such as matching to a photo on a driver's licence) and several mistakes were made.

There were no British dead and our plans for repatriating UK citizens never had to be realised. I received a letter of commendation for my advice on the complexities of recovering and identifying the victims of a disaster overseas. And after the Japanese tsunami, the government's chief scientific adviser was receptive to the idea that other voices, wider perspectives in government scientific advice, needed to be represented on SAGE – the 'soft intel' as the Cabinet Office called it. They saw the importance of including more people who understood the humanitarian aspects of emergencies and the needs of vulnerable people and children. And so this was briefly explored and trained. I was rolled out as a star turn at an internal Whitehall exercise for foreign diplomats as an example of the 'qualitative science' that would be allowed into SAGE, alongside the hard facts and cold figures. The delegates nodded and made notes and congratulated the UK on its bravery but I knew it would be hard to maintain.

Ultimately, spending time around these kinds of disasters shatters our human urge to believe we can bring complete order to any situation. We live in what disaster scientists call a 'high reliability/high risk world' and with every new technology, we introduce new ways to bring about our destruction. Nick was right to be frightened – some disasters are just too big. But life has to go on. It is not possible, or healthy, to live every day wondering how effective the control measures are at the nearest nuclear power station. It is completely natural, and psychologically healthy, for the human mind to turn itself away from these risks and not linger upon them. Could we really function day to day – raise babies, teach a class of children, drive a car, fly a plane – if we thought constantly about the risks we have chosen to tolerate?

We can take reasonable measures to keep ourselves safe but my work has also made me realise that every day without Armageddon is a good day. In my own disaster-themed versions of those brightly coloured life affirmations sold in card shops at railway stations, there is a huge part of me that believes in living for now, living for each day. We post memes to encourage each other to 'Live for the moment' or 'Dance in the rain' and one of my earliest lessons, taught by those who came before me, was that those who work regularly with death and disaster really, really do. Life really is to be lived as if it is precious, time-limited and so very fragile.

9

Ghost Train

On 6 July 2013, the town of Lac-Mégantic, Québec, was sweltering in the heat of summer. Jimmy Sirois and Marie Semie Alliance were struggling in their third-floor apartment. It was too hot for Marie's little girl, eighteen-month-old Milliana so they arranged for her to spend the night nearby at her grandmother's house, which had air conditioning. Jimmy and Marie stayed behind so they could be close to work. Their apartment block was fifty feet from the railway tracks that snaked around the town.

Just after 1 a.m., the brakes and couplings on a Montreal, Maine and Atlantic (MMA) train failed. It was carrying 7.7 million litres of petroleum crude oil in 72 tank cars. The train, which had been parked, unmanned, on a hill seven miles above the small town, slid down the hill, gaining speed until it exploded in the centre of the town. Residents described it as feeling like the end of the world and when the sun rose there was only fire and thick black smoke where there had once been buildings. Marie and Jimmy were among those who died in the fire and little Milliana's stars were changed forever.

The explosions and subsequent fires destroyed the historic town centre, causing the death of forty-seven local residents, many of whom were young and enjoying a night out at the local Musi-Café. Those killed, ages ranging from four to ninety-three, died in the downtown area of the city and their remains were consumed by a fire that reached temperatures beyond those used to cremate the human body.

The local residents had called these unmanned trains the ghost trains and safety concerns had been raised for years before. Immediate investigations found multiple safety breaches and in the following weeks, Transport Canada issued an emergency directive: from now on, no locomotive attached to one or more loaded tank cars could ever be left unattended on a main track. Locomotives left unattended on other tracks had to be locked. This time there were enough tombstones to bring about the change.

I never got to see the beauty of Lac-Mégantic before the disaster, to see this place when it was known as a jewel in Québec's crown. I saw it a year later, at its most vulnerable and broken. I was here to understand how we in the UK might recover and rebuild if we were to suffer an urban fire of this magnitude. I wanted to look at two things in particular: the weight given to and the role played by certainty of who the remains were and the wider path to some sense of a 'recovered' community. Then, most importantly, how these two were entangled.

I had tried to book my lodgings online: B&Bs by the lake, a motel in the town centre. I realised that the reason the web links kept failing was that the hotels no longer existed. The web pages were a teasing memory of a moment of time. On my first day there, I found a shop selling two separate calendars aimed at raising funds for the town. One showed the 'before' with an ice hockey game being played on the open streets, a row of fairy-lit boutiques and the Musi-Café before it was annihilated; the other showed the 'afterwards', with scenescapes of the ruined town, smoke rising above.[35] *Before* and *afterwards*. The two words that sum up the effects of disaster more than any others.

The first time that I came into the town, I came from the top and looked down, just as I did in Christchurch. There was a sharp incline down to the devastation, which only added to the startling optics. As far as I could strain to see, there were piles and piles of excavated dirt. The air was filled with the beeps of reversing trucks and still thick with the remnants of the benzene that had triggered the explosions. Benzene fumes sit heavily on clothes and in hair (the smell was still overpowering when I opened my suitcase back home). The fuel that had not ignited ran into the lake or burrowed into the water course. The flames had melted streetlights and reached temperatures high enough to split the rocks all the way down to the shoreline. The explosions in Lac-Mégantic were large enough to be captured by NASA and, as a disaster scene, the town's devastation was made for television. In fact, it was so brutally close to how

Hollywood depicts disaster that it was actually spliced into the popular Netflix film *Bird Box*. There was an apology but no removal of the footage that shows the hours after the fatal fire, tens of additional conflagrations lighting up the night sky.

The way to see a place after disaster is on foot. To follow the scars and the cleaves and the new contours created by kinetic energy of this magnitude. Walking around the immense site had been made easier for someone like me by the placing of flagged pathways and benches to sit on. From the start, they wanted people to come back, wanted people to know that they were trying to have something to see when you did.

One of the very first actions that all societies and civilisations demand at the scene of a disaster is that their dead are taken care of, and quickly. Sometimes the remains are heartbreakingly obvious. One set of human remains, a whole person fully carbonised, was visible on the main street for some hours after the incident, like one of the ash-casts created in Pompeii. Responders rushed to protect it and the other sets of fragile remains that lay nearby, exposed. But following a disaster, some of the dead stay hidden for much longer. And what happens when the dead become part of the ground and the dust and the scene, that will then also need to be recovered and then rebuilt? In Lac-Mégantic, remains had to be recovered from a number of settings, including apartments, but the largest number of deceased died together in the Musi-Café. Their remains were in a condition that anthropologists describe starkly as 'co-mingled'. The anthropologists took those bones, those 'cremains', to their laboratories and began a painstaking recovery process.

In the first few months after a disaster, a lot of effort goes into simply surviving and getting through. Then external pressures start to pile up. Central and local government, the public, village elders want to start the clear up. This is an inevitable flashpoint of tension. It will always feel too soon and like forgetting to the bereaved, the survivors and the frontline first respond-ers. 'This is our place, not theirs,' a grieving family raged to me about somewhere they considered to be a grave for their loved one, after an architect's draw-ing of a memorial garden, produced for a government contract, was sent to them. This transition is also diffi-cult because it is the moment a disaster site becomes home to the unresting dead, with no more chance of life. In the weeks following the attacks on the Twin Towers there were physical altercations at the Ground Zero site. Responders, overcome with emotion, were aghast that they were being pulled off a site where they still clung on to the shred of hope that their fire station brothers might be found alive. They swung punches at those moving them on.

As in New York in 2001 and London in 2005, forensic anthropologists took the lead in much of the identification work in Lac Mégantic. Crucially for the world of disaster victim identification, anthros are ideal for fast-triaging whether a bone is animal or human. There are chemical tests on the proteins that can be done but nothing can match for speed the stinging, sarcastic response delivered by a senior anthro to a detective who presents her with a cow bone. The main characteristic of remains at the Lac-Mégantic site was the level of burning. Burned skeletal remains are a regular occurrence in anthro labs, ranging from the grand – war criminals ordering petrol to be poured into the mass grave – to the local – domestic murders covered up through the use of accelerants. So many of the remains I have seen have been assaulted by fire. Sometimes it was all that would come into the Iraq mortuary. The body contorted into what is called the pugilistic pose, the stance of a boxer, caused by the shrinkage and contracture of muscles.

But the physics of the Lac-Mégantic explosions meant that the temperatures had exceeded those usually seen in a crematorium, removing most tissue and coalescing the minerals within bone to form only sharp crystals that could turn to dust in the most careful of gloved hands. The 'friable cremains' as they are known forensically require very gentle handling. They are a staple part of forensic anthropology training because they present such a challenge. The thermal effects on the bone also create little fractures that make analysing criminal actions by a perpetrator close to impossible.

Anthros understand that the communities they work with need an end point. They also understand the perils that DNA testing brings and, like me, were becoming acutely attuned to its risks as well as its strengths. The question of whether perpetual DNA testing created harm in post-disaster and conflict settings had become a staple theme at forensic anthropology and human rights conferences – earlier that year, I had attended an international event in The Hague on exactly that issue.

I went to Montreal to meet Renée Kosalka, who had honed her craft, like so many of the best forensic anthropologists, in war graves. She had spent years piecing together the remains left by the conflict in Yugoslavia. Renée was based in a laboratory in the bowels of the Montreal police headquarters, which was straight out of an edgy Danish drama – imposing architecture and clanging gates. My rucksack and I queued conspicuously to be scanned and searched by handsome, strong-jawed policemen. The laboratory offices were a contrast to the sterile corridors: jumbled desks, favourite mugs, photos of teams at digs in Rwanda and Kosovo pinned to noticeboards. Piles of research papers and those little 'you have a phone message' sticky notes. These labs are literally straight out of a Kathy Reichs thriller as the crime writer holds a consulting position here. She has a chair and a desk kept vacant for her. It was decorated with photos and the dust jackets from her books and a sign 'Reserved for the Queen of Crime Fiction'. I was not sure that her hard-working colleagues in the lab were being entirely supportive.

For weeks after the disaster, Renée worked in the hot sun – Lac-Mégantic was thirty-seven degrees by then – with her work shrouded by fencing and tarpaulin. She worked in the downtown area of the city, the crude oil fire's ground zero, to excavate the remains and separate them from each other before transporting them, tenderly, to her lab. She tended to fourteen diffcrent scenes in total. Though by the time I met her, she was already working on the aftermath of a second mass fatality fire under her care, while still writing up reports and performing further tests for the Lac-Mégantic deceased.[36] The ebb and flow of two disasters was visibly all around her.

It was Renée's job to reunite the tiny fragments left of a person. This re-articulation, this placing of rib fragment with tooth with foot bone, is a lengthy, sensitive and confronting process. Unlike the attacks in London and NewYork, there were no terrorist remains to remove. This was simply about placing as much of the person back together as possible so they could be returned to their families and laid to rest. Renée had agreed three months as her timescale. One family member, frustrated with the time the process was taking, spoke up at a public meeting, saying, 'I don't mind if I get them back with other people mixed in there – I just want them back!' As he spoke, there was a gasp and some of the other families looked horrified. 'It was the mothers,' said Renée. 'You could see it on the face of the mothers ... They wanted just *their* child back, no one else's remains.'

The responders were protective of the remains and wanted to keep them close but a small sample of each of the remains did leave Québec. The Lac-Mégantic investigators tipped their hat to the growing Western obsession with pushing DNA testing boundaries by sending three sets of small, carefully managed samples to laboratories at Thunder Bay, Canada; the International Commission for Missing Persons Laboratories in Bosnia and the Office of Chief Medical Examiner (OCME), New York City. The responders[37] asserted strongly that these were simply to *test* the process, to *confirm* what could be found. This was an important difference to 9/11 and placed a semantic and emotional boundary on the process that constant testing in a laboratory would not be happening to the deceased here. Their own results in their own Montreal laboratories had yielded exactly the same results at an earlier stage.

At Lac-Mégantic, the strategy for the response was set and written down early on. It did something that I had not seen before. It stated that the first aim of the response was to identify, yes, but it then added a second goal: *to ensure the remains would rest*. Responders had thought clearly about what the recovery should look like. What ten years' time should look like for both the families and the community. They knew that for this community to rest, then their intervention with the dead of the disaster needed resolution. They set about building this goal into everything they went on to do.

The ossuary for the remains that could not be identified is carved into the shape of an angel and sits prominently within Lac Mégantic's main cemetery at the bottom of a slight slope. She can be seen from any number of angles within the municipal graveyard, which contains the individual graves too. Families were given the option to opt out (with some limitations) of the identification process and allow all of their loved one's remains to rest in the ossuary. It was explained to them that the coroner's office would retain a sample from the compartments in the ossuary so that if the technology changed they could do a test but the ossuary would stay undisturbed. The coroners did not want to have to return to the families repeatedly with requests to exhume or re-bury or re-open family tombs within the large graveyard that casts an eye over the lake on one side and another eye over the downtown area. They had heard the stories from New York, of the sometimes many funerals for the same person as more remains were identified, and were worried about putting their community through that.

Eating lunch in Lac-Mégantic's brand new Metro supermarket, one week after it opened, I asked the emergency planner from the council if they thought Lac-Mégantic could have done all this – all this re-covering and regeneration, the Halloween parade, the new downtown area, the identically rebuilt Musi-Café, the memorial archways, the plans for a conference centre – if the identification process had been very visibly ongoing. If every lorryload of clay was still being sifted in a central location while families waited for an undefined end point some time in the future. The responder replied with emphasis and arm waving. '*Non, non, non.* The thought of this going on for another five years ... terrible! None of this [the regeneration work] could ever have happened. People needed an end point.'

Of all the disasters and the identification of the disaster dead I have seen, Lac-Mégantic felt the most calm and the most gentle. The coroners' handling of the Lac-Mégantic ossuary is one of the most potent examples of the way that responders can use foresight of future harm in their forensic approach. It was also the only place where I heard it explicitly expressed that there was a link between the decisions made in the response and what happens next for a community. The relatives and friends of those lost, the community, may not know any different – they may think that this is always the way things are done. Only people like me knew what was being fought for behind closed doors.

There are not teams and teams of scientists working on this every day as there still are in New York. In Lac-Mégantic, the scientists watch, they wait, they are ready if they are needed in the future. But the parents of those people dancing in a café have held their funeral and do not wait for a knock at the door to say another minute sample has been found.

Even as it segued into a building site, Lac-Mégantic stayed as a hopeful place, with activities and events, and a constant belief that they would come back from this. The importance of the children's voices was central and to commemorate the first anniversary, the children and young people of this place had made a video set to the song 'Happy' by Pharrell Williams.[38] Many of the places and spaces that housed that first year of recovering are captured on screen, combined with dancing and singing.

'As soon as it happened,' Marie-Claude, adviser to the mayor explained, 'People started to come back . . . people who had moved away to go to college and then stayed away. They came home. The place is full of young people again. It was their friends who died in the Musi-Café. They came home to honour them.'

A memorial has limited utility. It acts as totemic reminder, yes, and as a place to provoke thought and contemplation. It has historical significance. But Lac-Mégantic taught me that perhaps the greater honour for those who died is to live for them.

To keep their stories alive by including them in yours.

IO

Sunflowers

The hospital staff gathered excitedly around Tom to ask questions. It is a scene that has become familiar to me throughout our marriage. People love a pilot, the uniform and the status, and perhaps there will always be something magician-like about the ability to make a big hulking metal tube take off from the ground. 'What routes do you fly?' the anaesthetist asked and then a nurse piped up with, 'I've always wanted to know, why can't planes reverse?' They chatted on for some time while I lay flat on my back, fixing on a grubby ceiling tile, until the consultant clapped her hands and said exuberantly, 'So! To business.'

The business was me and also would soon be Mabel, who was about to be cut from my womb. They ran through their pre-op checklists, adding in 'doors to manual' for Tom's benefit, with a giggle. Eight minutes later, all nine pounds of her was here and, like her older sister, she was perfect and worth the wait.

Two months later, July 2014, I found myself having a heated debate with a police officer. The UK's Disaster

Victim Identification unit were training together at a hotel in Yorkshire. I had become worried that the scenarios in our training were too easy, beginning with a number of assumptions that essentially made life simpler for the responders. One of these was that they would always be greatly assisted by a cheery collaboration of Interpol responders and unfettered access to the scene.

I had attended a number of the international DVI events held annually at the Interpol headquarters in Lyon and, like most disaster soirees, they were upbeat events bolstered with large amounts of food and wine. A champagne toast to our hosts and a commemorative photograph on the steps. But I felt this dulled our senses and our sharp elbows for the realities of the taut state of international relations in many parts of the world. Kenyon had been a much better introduction to that. Not only did they hold military support contracts but there were many tales of inhibited access to scenes when commercial air crashes had occurred close to contested air space and even war zones. They had once been given twenty-five minutes to retrieve a hundred fragmented bodies from a jungle plane crash. Hurling limbs and tissue into body bags and running for their lives. This speedy retrieval is known as a 'scoop and run'.

For this training, I had developed an exercise in which a UK passenger plane has been shot down over conflicted territories. I wanted our focus to be on the families of the missing and how we would brief them on the complexities of the DVI process in such tense circumstances. I launched the scenario but I was losing the debate, with a senior detective scolding me for always looking for negatives. A female detective who had always mentored me passed me a note on a biscuit wrapper as she saw my face colour and body give away my frustration. It said, 'Just because they disagree with you, doesn't mean you are wrong.' I suggested a tea break.

There was a wall-mounted TV tuned to the BBC News channel above the coffee machines and the little packets of individually wrapped biscuits. A breaking news banner came across the TV screen. A Malaysia Air Boeing 777 on a flight from Amsterdam to Kuala Lumpur had been hit by a missile as it flew over rebel-held territory in Ukraine.[39] There were 283 passengers and 15 crew members on board. The edges of the room faded away as they always do and my vision was fixed entirely on the TV screen.

'It won't have any British on it,' remarked one of my colleagues through a mouthful of shortbread. Then his mobile phone started to ring.

Soon afterwards, mine started to ring too, and for once it wasn't work. I was needed at home, urgently. Just a few weeks after the birth of Mabel, Tom had been booked in for an urgent tonsillectomy. He didn't recover well and, silently, viciously, a nasty infection had crept into the wound. He was off work, vacillating between bed and sofa, while we adjusted to life as a four. He was in severe pain and spent the post-operative period just wanting to sleep, irritated and sensitive to the noise around him. And there was a lot of noise. Two months after the birth, and two weeks after his op, I had been booked to co-deliver this training. I had taken a gamble, strapped myself into some post-partum leggings and booked the train. I reasoned that I was only about 90 minutes from home if Tom needed me and left a trail of food and kids' toys and DVDs. This was important training and I told myself I needed to be there.

But now Tom was ringing me himself to tell me he was sorry to have bothered me but he had called 999 and that when I got home there might be a bit of a mess. He had had a huge arterial bleed from his throat and into his mouth. Disorientated from pain, fear and blood loss, he had roamed around the house, losing large quantities of red blood and black tissue amongst the soft furnishings. At its most dramatic, the artery had simply spurted continuously into the various receptacles that Tom had tried to hold to his face.

Like our parents and grandparents before us, we had by now stretched our financial resources to obtain a mortgage on a money pit in a rural village in Nottinghamshire. Every bit of spare cash went on new windows and insulation and floorboards. Tom had spent the previous nine months refurbishing our kitchen. He had sourced stone for the floor and laid it himself. It was burnished and beautiful and now coated in thick arterial spray.

My colleagues at the hotel got me into a taxi. The childminder had managed to get to the house before the ambulance had pulled away and had taken the children to her home. Soon after my arrival at the emergency department of the hospital, Tom was rushed into the operating theatre for surgery and cauterisation. He had lost an awful lot of his blood volume from a severe post-tonsillectomy haemorrhage. This is a rare complication, though much more likely when adults have the op than when children do, and the bleeding can be very hard to stop. The area where the tonsils are is supplied by five different arteries. An infection in the wound site will trigger bleeding; the arteries continue to bleed and in some cases, this after-effect proves fatal. Many coroners have since regaled me with their own experiences of post-tonsillectomy fatalities and their inquests.

I wanted to punch the nurse who said to me, 'We are going to try to do everything we can for him.' Because that was what they said on the TV when all hope was lost. There was nothing else I could do but wait. The gurney and the floor around were covered in my husband's blood. It was on me and on my shoes. A number of religions place huge value on blood – our entire life force is within it and God is within it; it belongs to God. I don't know about that but one thing you notice when it is spread everywhere is just how bright a red it is. When I arrived at the hospital, Tom's clothes had all been cut off to get to his vital areas. He was naked and exposed. My man, a foot taller than me and my protector, lay open and vulnerable. While I stood helpless, nurses had climbed across him and rubbed on his sternum to try to rouse him and I remember thinking that they could not have known that they were rubbing on the area that he and I called his chest wig. It was a massive sprouting, porn-star bush of hair that had grown suddenly and lustily in his twenties. I loved nestling into it at the end of a long hard day. It was his smell. It was him. I knew that if they returned him to me dead, then it would feel different, smell different, be different. Then he was whisked away to the operating theatre.

As the nurses cleared up around me, noisily raising and dropping the lids on clinical waste bins, I assumed that I was now a widow. I thought about the hymns that Tom might want at the likely well-attended funeral and the right phrases to use when asking his parents to get here. Should I tell them now that he was dead? Or was it kinder to let them think that he was seriously ill, let them do the four-hour drive and then tell them once they could sit down and I could get them sweet tea? I thought about the best picture to release to any press enquiries. I knew that the airline would say nice things about him. They might send people in uniform to sit around me at the crematorium.

While cleaning staff, called hastily to the cubicle, started to mop the floor around me I berated myself for not pushing each of the nurses out of the way and climbing across Tom myself, one last time before the surgeons took him. Breathing him in, burying my hands in his hair, and holding him while he still had his life spark and before the grey came.

At that point, I realised that they had put all of Tom's clothes into the clinical waste bin. Shredded fabric and his leather deck shoes. But they had kept his watch and a rucksack in white bin liners that were now stained red. They had decided these things would have value and the other items should be waste. I mused on the choice of the white bin bag. I empathised with the Hobson's choices; no right answer there. A black bin bag looks like rubbish – families hate that. In a clear bag, items are too obvious and visible, which can be very distressing. A white bag shows the blood starkly but at least it hides the objects. Or maybe it was any bag that day that was on the shelf.

I pushed my way through the nurses who had worked for two hours to save my husband and started to lift every last shred of Tom out of the bin. The shoes were not just covered with blood but actually partially filled: blood was sloshing in them. I was definitely a widow now. Nobody could survive losing so much blood that it can be tipped about in your shoe, like a gravy boat. As I rummaged deeper and deeper into the bin, I thought about the ZAKA, the Israeli disaster body recovery teams.[40] This male-only voluntary organisation was formed in 1995 by Orthodox Jews and has been kept continuously busy deploying to suicide bombings in Israel. According to Orthodox Jewish customs, their responders try to recover each and every body fragment, ensuring none of the person is left behind. In practical terms, this means that they gather up every possible piece of tissue and organ after a bomb or shooting, using little pieces of cloth and sponges to soak up every bit of fluid and chipping away at road surfaces to ensure that no viscera is embedded there. The water used to wash the scene is kept too. I had been to UK DVI training sessions where our police had discussed potential terrorism attacks on a synagogue and the need to make sure we had a supply of those little sponges. Most of the responders looked troubled at this point, thinking about the practicalities: where could we get the sponges from so quickly and who would we call to let us dig up the road?

Until that minute, in a grubby cubicle in Doncaster Royal Infirmary, I had thought the approach of ZAKA was a little excessive. But now it made perfect sense. None of my love was to find his way into the bin. I would have kept the cleaner's water if I had not thought that the nurses might have me sectioned under mental health legislation for trying. One nurse asked me to step away from the bin. She told me firmly that those items were waste and I should leave them. 'It's OK,' I said calmly. 'This is my job. I know what I am doing.'

I put every last bit of Tom into the white bags and called a taxi. I was certain that I was a widow and all I wanted was to get back to the children. Propelled by adrenaline I made my way to a mini cab waiting at the hospital entrance, the driver of which kept stealing glances in his rear-view mirror at the strange, grim-faced, silent woman clutching two bloody white bin liners. Yup, definitely a new widow. I saw him take in the blood on my face and my shirt sleeves.

I felt a sense of detachment as I watched him watching me in this dark place. I had felt something similar in childbirth and in miscarriage. I do it at funerals and when making love. Now this is interesting, says half of my brain, while the other half screams at it just to live in the moment. To love. Laugh. Live. Bleed. Hurt. Come. But even in that moment, I was thinking about disaster and how I was luckier than most to have had the chance to say goodbye.

By the time I was home, and my babies were fed and in bed, the adrenaline had worn off and I was incapable of even moving. When my dad found me, I was curled up in a ball of the white bags on the floor of the sitting room in the dark.

He took a call from the hospital: Tom was in intensive care. Saved, stitched and transfused.

The next morning, Dad took Elizabeth to nursery school and settled Mabel in her cot before bustling around the kitchen to make lunch. Jay had dropped in groceries and put his head around the corner of my office. 'Eh up, Luce. Need owt?' And then headed out again. It was time for me to go back to work.

Bodies, and their parts, have been items to barter with for as long as there have been wars. There are carefully brokered arrangements governed by the International Red Cross and Red Crescent for scenes of conflict all over the world, so that local aid workers can recover the bodies of soldiers and civilians. But sometimes they would be given just minutes to grab as many pieces as possible. I could not shake the implications of that from my scenario planning.

The loss of MH17 proved I was right to be nervous about scene access. Again my 'soft intel' was backed by a number of recent observations. The international diplomatic networks, essential for DVI to work properly, had been fraying and this would always have an impact on disaster response. I have worked on air disasters that involved 37 different nationalities and their embassies. There had been a number of early warning signs. A year before the loss of MH17, the Somali militant group Al-Shabaab laid siege to a Nairobi shopping mall. Shoppers from several different countries had been caught up in the attack and I had attended the Interpol briefing to UK DVI that suggested that relations between the nations involved had become strained. There had been tense little power struggles about intelligence sharing and about identification; the Germans and the Israeli security operatives were attempting to outfox each other for access to the terrorists' vehicles in the car park. Too-soon media briefings had vastly inflated the number of terrorists and misidentified a young boy as one of the hostage takers.

There was also a particular challenge for the UK responders that I spotted creeping in. The UK DVI team were good at what they did but they were occasions when they caused other nations to bristle. I wondered if some nations found us a little too smug and a little too quick and keen to deploy. Our requests to attend some scenes where British citizens had been killed overseas had been rejected several times. In 2012, following a plane crash that killed seven British men, the heads of Nepalese police and forensic teams told the press that they could manage 'perfectly well' without any British deployment. I also wondered sometimes if our approach to human tissue, with its strict legislation, seemed a bit worthy and scolding at times. Did it look like we had forgotten the overall goal, which was to identify the remains? As in the 2004 tsunami, our foreign counterparts would regularly remove jaws and hands, or even complete sets of organs. Occasionally I would watch in interest as their own citizens discovered an organ scandal like Alder Hey somewhere within their health system. Their tissue approach would usually be quietly reformed soon after.

The majority of the MH17 wreckage had come down in sunflower fields in the heart of the conflict zone. Diplomats and policing responders at the highest level were working to gain access to the scene and fractious negotiations were underway to find some way in. The Russians appeared keen to heap some additional humiliation onto Western nations and the rumour was that they had stated that any international responder found speaking in an English or American accent, or wearing the uniforms of those nations, would be shot. But they would briefly tolerate the Dutch and the Australians. So our finest intelligence sources took the decision to send a Welshman and dress him up as an Australian.

As it turned out, scene access was almost non-existent but a cohort of Ukrainian miners had been dispatched to gather the deceased. The location of each body part was marked with a wooden stick and a white flag. 'My God,' exclaimed one of the

British civil servants in horror, on hearing this. 'They're sending in children!' The Foreign and Commonwealth Office had confused a vowel and thought they had deployed minors.

The phone rang and as I scrambled to take the call in my office, I leaned heavily against the door to shut out the sound of children's TV. Tom was asleep upstairs. After some intense global diplomacy, it had been agreed that the bodies from MH17 would be taken to the Netherlands before being identified and returned to their respective countries.[41] My mission was to make sure that whatever had happened at the scene in Ukraine itself, our treatment of the bodies once they were returned would comply as closely as possible with Lord Clarke's recommendations.

'You need to open the coffins back here in the UK. You have to check for personal effects.' I had no time for introductions to the topic.

'For fuck's sake, Lucy, every bloody time . . .' Dave is a friend but I am also aware that he finds me intensely frustrating. He is a police officer focused on the difficult business of identifying victims' bodies and often sees my commitment to the personal effects and the wider issues relating to the care of families as a distraction in the early hours. He can get as angry as he likes with me in the moment because I always know we will work it out later, and that underneath it all he is one of the most compassionate people I have ever met.

'I've just had this out with our guy in COBR and the military liaison. There are no bloody personal effects. It's all gone, looted. It's a fucking war zone, Lucy.'

I pressed on. 'But you've got the Red Cross in there? They'll try and keep some of it safe? What did you take off them in the mortuary? And there might be items in the coffins—'

'Look.' He took a big breath in. 'We can't open the coffins.'

I knew why. The MH17 bodies had been treated with liberal amounts of the chemical formalin before being put on a train in Ukraine. By the time the deceased reached the specially constructed mortuary in the Netherlands, the responders had to declare a major chemical incident due to the levels of embalming chemicals. Work had to be stopped while they were fitted for full breathing apparatus and the strength of the chemicals used caused ongoing problems for the responders. It also made viewing of the deceased by the families much more difficult.

My next conversation was with the coroner. The coroner assigned to MH17 was Catherine, one of the cadre, the group of twelve coroners I had been allowed to advise and train throughout my career. She would be the one to carry the can if any mistakes were made in the DVI process. She is cut from the same cloth as my aunty and uncle and fiercely protective of the dead that come into her care and the rights and protections of the families. Like me, she always has her well-thumbed copy of Lord Clarke's report in her wheelie bag.

Catherine was on a tea break from a meeting at the highest levels of government. She had just gone head to head with the prime minister, David Cameron, who wanted a military repatriation via Brize Norton for the deceased of MH17. She had fought back hard. This approach looks good for pomp and ceremony but is disastrous for creating a false sense of certainty. It allows the families to believe that the right person is coming back. Instead, what we needed, for the families, was to be able to take our time with the body when it got back here. Catherine needed to be able to know who and what she was getting back. She was ready for anything. Some countries hollow out their deceased, packing them with straw, and use their organs for training or just throw them away. They also have very different views on preserving the personal effects.

We discussed the best way to conduct the identification and what the challenges would be. Catherine had already decided to arrange for a 'digital autopsy' – CT scanning of the deceased. This is sometimes lobbied for by faith groups as it is much less invasive to the body. It is also ideal for contaminated incidents because the deceased can be lifted out of the coffin and scanned while still inside the body bag.

We moved on to the certainty of identification. The international message was that while the situation in Ukraine might have been fraught, once the bodies were taken to the Netherlands all deceased would be identified to the same standard. Committees had been formed to ensure and safeguard it. Dave was a member. We were told there was no need for other countries to initiate their own processes. But that level of trust had let us down before. And Catherine wanted to open the coffins. She wanted to be able to tell the families her own truth, not a second-hand version. She wanted to reassure them that her own team of pathologists and APTs had laid eyes on their loved ones.

Catherine went back into the meeting, thanking me for my reassurance. She planned to tell the PM what she wanted and that she expected him to pay for it.

'Wish me luck,' she chuckled.

Catherine won both battles that day. By allowing her teams to open the coffins, she was able to arrange further, reassuring checks on the identification of the deceased. She was also able to ascertain whether there were any personal effects in the coffins that the families could then have returned if they so wished. She managed to ensure that the bodies were repatriated quietly on civilian flights so that she could ensure that the families were not 'mis-sold' an incorrect identity before she had had a chance to confirm.

The Russians continued to deny investigators safe access to the MH17 scene and to the debris. However, a Sky News reporter did manage to gain access to the fields and, in actions that he later described as a 'serious error of judgement', appeared to rummage through the passengers' belongings in a live broadcast, holding items like a drink's flask up to the camera. I could not bear to watch the screen and reached for the remote. I was in our bedroom, checking on Tom. 'Leave it on,' Tom said, gripped, as if watching a horror film. And then quietly, 'Where will it all go now?'

At that point, I wasn't sure. Later, it was confirmed that the International Red Cross had moved quickly to rescue whatever they could in the first days after the crash and wherever possible these items made their way back to the families of the deceased. And then, over the next nine months, burnt passports, books, glasses and jewellery were found by responders retracing their steps in the farmer's fields and by families making pilgrimage. A foot and other body parts were handed over to the investigators. An air crash into soil can burrow the main cabin five metres into the ground and personal effects can be lost deep in the earth into which they landed. In a horrible extra after-effect, personal belongings will be yielded over a period of time by weather or by farming, revealing themselves after rainfall or landslide.

Or, in the case of MH17, whenever a field of sunflowers was ploughed.

11

The Rollercoaster

An ability to conduct a hyper-rapid risk assessment of a situation, otherwise known as gut instinct, is often undervalued in our very modern world. It is hard to articulate and often involves feelings more than words. It is linked to lightning-fast reactions in the brain and the production of chemicals like adrenaline and cortisol. It involves klaxons in the head, sweaty palms, rapid breathing and a whole load of feelings centred around the gut. And more specifically the bowels. The Ancient Greeks considered the bowels the centre of our emotional responses and the connection between the mind and the gut has been explored throughout the history of medicine.[42]

The use of instinctive responses is not actually impetuous or irrational. It is closely linked to our preexisting knowledge bases and set of life experiences. These experiences help us to interpret tiny little environmental breadcrumbs as subtle cues. Our instincts can be honed through use and experience. And you reach a point in life where they are usually right. 'You can ignore me,' I said at a meeting recently, 'but you

would be wrong!' And of course as I said it I grinned
and then broke into laughter to remove any accusation
of arrogance or hubris – an old habit from many
years of being on charm offensive as one of the only
women in the room. Colleagues laughed along with
me. But a few noted the steely look in my eyes. I
meant it.

I have met so many survivors of fatal incidents
who have wondered at exactly what forces propelled
them out of the fire or the aircraft cabin or train
carriage. They have no knowledge or memory of
reaching the scorched scrub at the side of the
runway or the railway embankment. I have also met
several people whose relationships have irretriev-
ably broken down as a result: one partner unable to
understand how the love of their life scrambled
over eight other rows of seats in thick black smoke,
leaving them behind, without looking back. They
struggle to forgive what appears to be gross
abandonment and neglect, without consideration
of those most earthly of instincts. Only when you
understand the role of the amygdala in the brain,
that propels our fight or flight reactions, do these
'override' reactions make sense – the reactions that
power our limbs to move or to lift are not conscious
but primitive ones. In some industries, these feelings are given more tangible weight and credence.
In aviation, they are wrapped up within the concept
of 'cockpit resource management'[43] and the meaning and interpretation of these instincts and hyper
assessments are studied as 'human factors'. Tom's

mantra is, 'Where there is doubt, there is no doubt.' If your spidey senses are telling you to abort the landing, you do it. No questions asked. (Unless you fly for a roguish budget airline, where lots of questions may be asked.) If you think you need to call a May Day, you call it.

Of course, our instincts are tinged with the bias of hindsight. So many eye witnesses to disaster have a tale of delaying or taking a different route moments before. Tube bombing survivors who recount, time and again, how a voice in their head told them to swap seats. 'That bloody voice,' chuckled one detective to me after his ninetieth witness statement. 'I hope I remember to listen to mine when the time comes.' It can be hard to differentiate between intuition, just before, and a very rapid assessment of an emerging situation, just after, and an attempt after the fact to make sense of the random cruelty of disasters. Not to mention survivor's bias – the fact that we only hear the stories of those who made it. It can also be tactless because for every survivor who did move away from the window, there is a bereaved family who could choose to interpret that discussion as their loved one lacking the instinctive reactions necessary to protect themselves.

Women in disaster planning and response are constantly accused of overreaction, of too much thinking and emotion. We ignore our instincts in an effort to fit in. I was regularly counselled on keeping quiet or playing the game. Squashing down the intuition. Some of the times I have felt most betrayed is when a fellow woman, possibly one of only three or four in a meeting of twenty people, has sidled up to me at the end to whisper that she agrees with my articulated fears but cannot risk outwardly advocating for them. She does not want to look 'hysterical'. Even our own biology conspires against us in emergency planning. Right up until the 1950s, female hysteria was considered common and chronic in those with a womb. It was enough to have women locked away. Though the specified range of symptoms – including anxiety, fear and a 'tendency to cause trouble for others'[44] – might actually be thought of as assets in our trade. My female colleagues and I would talk about it among ourselves. How do you manage the feelings that something very bad was about to happen or was very 'off' without being accused of being 'emotional'? What to do with a barrage of firing synapses that you know you will ignore at your peril?

All of which is how I found myself sitting with a baby and a toddler, next to an overflowing waste bin, with every sinew of my body telling me to run.

One way that I have always tried to 'yin' the 'yang' of my work with disasters, is to book in nice things for the weekend. These plans are often derailed and I have learned over the years to dial down any excesses and manage my expectations. But I still occasionally get led astray. Which is why, in the spring of 2015, when I spotted an advert for the grand opening of tree house-style lodges at Alton Towers theme park, despite a knot in my bowels about the cost, I decided to book one for a night. We could do CBeebies Land with the kids and the main theme park, and it also gave us access to the swimming pool.

The reality compared to my imagination was stark. The nerves of both children and husband were frayed by the long drive and within a few minutes of entering the 'tropical' water land, we were evacuated back to the changing rooms due to a 'faeces-related incident' in the toddler pool. We quickly called it a day at CBeebies Land after Mabel screamed all the way past the Teletubbies and the Octonauts. We decided to attempt one more activity before heading back for a pub meal and some nap time in the lodge. The girls and I would watch Tom on one of the big boy rollercoasters.

Alton Towers had been my Graceland growing up. Two hours from Birkenhead, it was the Neverland of high school trips, or a very rare luxury proffered by a brave Girl Guiding leader. The park is all bright primary colours and beautiful lawned gardens. The air is thick with the smell of sugared doughnuts and pure, juvenile thrills. I had linked arms with a boy for the first time at this place.

But on this visit in 2015, the park seemed tired. There was rubbish and some of the signage had been allowed to fade and fall off. One of the ways that instinct and intuition intersect with more tangible cues and evidence is through the visible representations of a 'safety culture' in a place. It is something that is often discussed in disaster management. Bluntly, it is about first impressions.

When you walk into somewhere that feels, looks and smells clean, where people are smiling and look like they care, it is more likely to be safe. This was first explored and defined in reviews of the Chernobyl disaster and describes how safety is a 'culture' within an organisation where every part of the system contributes. I always note how easy a place is to navigate, where the fire exits are and if the lifts are working.

In after-disaster inquiries and reports these little dots are often joined up to expose near misses and early warning signs. It is rare to find an organisation that fails catastrophically out of the blue with no problems in other areas too. It's why when I am trying to get a handle on an organisation, I will often arrive early and spend some time undercover (not in a Jason Bourne way – people just tend to assume I am lost and looking for the coffee shop). One of the most worrying signs of a degrading safety culture is when you can hear staff openly discussing how bad things are.

Tom wanted to try out the new ride, The Smiler – fourteen loops making it one of the most looped rollercoasters in the world. The queue for it was a long one so Tom reluctantly joined the shorter queue for the Rita rollercoaster, with fewer loops, instead. It was a hot June day but it was also incredibly windy and the tops of the rollercoaster looked fragile and buffeted. I told myself not to be silly as I fought the urge to grab Tom's arm and tell him that we needed to go now. We waited nearby as Tom edged further up the queue and both children started to cry. Elizabeth was screaming that she didn't want Tom to go any further and Mabel was screaming because it was too windy for me to pour her mushed food pouch into her plastic bowl. To get more purchase on the puree, I sheltered as close as I could get to the protective fencing around Rita. Rust from her metalwork dripped onto the pram and children cried as she creaked ominously. I nudged the litter away that was spilling out of the unemptied bins with my feet to clear them a picnic area. Eventually, we were joined by a wind-battered Tom, who looked a bit sick. 'That was a bit hairy,' he said. 'Let's go.'

As we left the park and made our way back to our lodge, I started to notice the looks on the staff's faces had changed. They were wearing the same set expressions that I have seen many times on police and airline staff, that day on the London Underground and in Bristol's student union many years before. The air was still a cacophony of excited squeals but there was a stave of different, more urgent shouts running over the top. And as we walked, the park staff started to run the other way, past us and towards the rollercoasters we had just left.

Moments earlier – at 1.51 p.m. on 2 June 2015 – a series of failings meant that four carriages packed with people on The Smiler rollercoaster slammed into an empty carriage still on the track. The Smiler was still running in 46mph winds, despite guidance saying it should not operate in speeds greater than 34mph. Undergoing the same forces of a 90mph car crash, the passengers who bore the worst of the impact suffered severe injuries, including amputations to lower limbs and massive blood loss. The emergency services' later evidence reported that they had found the site inaccessible and hard to navigate. Merlin Entertainment, the park owners, admitted a series of health and safety breaches and were fined £5 million and strongly criticised by the judge at the trial for trying to shift blame to park employees. It was noted that in the judgement the owners had allowed the breaches to develop for a period of time, and the court emphasised how serious the failings were. Merlin apologised for 'letting people down, with devastating consequences'.

It took six hours for the most severely injured passengers to be extricated from the carriages. Tom put the children to bed. I sat miserably in our strange little fake tree house listening to the sounds of the air ambulance landing and taking off. The excited squeals had long since stopped and been replaced by the high-pitched gnaw of metal-cutting saws and ambulance sirens.

As it grew dark, somebody pushed a letter under our door from the management saying that the park would now close immediately 'following a dreadful incident'. There was a number to contact if we needed help and the cost of the woodland lodge had been refunded to my credit card.

*   *   *

Colleagues have often ribbed me that while it made sense for me to see so much chaos as a responder, to have also encountered what seems to be so many disasters as a citizen must be disconcerting. When I told them I'd been at Alton Towers that day, some of the DVI team teased that they would start calling me 'Jonah' – in honour of the maritime superstition that there was one person on board the boat who caused bad luck for the voyage.

But I have never thought of it like that. We all live with 'when' not 'if'. Tragedies happen around us every day. People marvel at being in both a plane crash and a car crash as extraordinarily bad luck, when in fact the statistics clearly indicate that this is both possible and likely. We also misinterpret risk data that says '1 in 1,000 people', or 'once in 100 years' to mean that the fates spread risk fairly. In fact, the same person can be hit over and over again. I often wonder whether our recent ancestors, who would have seen fires and floods, mining disasters and disease, infant mortality and injury as a constant, would find our denial about life's frailty extraordinary.

We also have a tendency to notice the bad coincidences but not the infinite number of good coincidences that happen in equal magnitude to us every day. The stars that align to mean somebody can fall in love at a bus stop or reacquaint with the best friend from nursery school in an airport lounge. The miracle of biological coincidences that is the conception of a baby. The times that the plane or the car didn't crash.

So, in the end, when I have been caught up – albeit on the periphery – in disasters, I don't find it extraordinary. Why wouldn't it have been us who were there that day?

12

Safe Hands

Tom had been up for most of the night, preparing. And so had I. At 6 a.m., he stepped in the shower while I made him a cup of tea. Our two babies, aged four and one, woke and then began to play noisily in the kitchen. It was 27 June 2015, just three and a half weeks after the major incident at Alton Towers.

He dressed in silence and then packed his work bag. On a work morning, he never deviated from the same ritual, patting his blazer pockets to check that his keys and his work mobile were in the right place. From the gangly student I first met he has weathered into a seasoned aviator and the airline's youngest trainer of other captains. He reminds me of Tom Hanks playing Chesley Sullenberger in the movie *Sully*. When I met him he had a halo of blond curls that he would try to corral into a Huffman Aviation baseball cap. They have long since receded, leaving behind a hairline that earned him the nickname of 'Prince William' in his crew room. He is still a contained man of few words. We could not be more different. Each other's counterpoint. I enjoy our silences, companionable and restorative. So no words isn't unusual for him but on this morning the silence was pained. Dressed in his full uniform, he walked towards the kitchen door and then stopped still. He put his black leather work bag down firmly on the floor and looked at me, stricken.

I opened my mouth to reassure him but before I could speak Elizabeth appeared behind him and said, 'Hey Dad, you need to get to work, people are waiting for you to give them their smile back.' Nine months earlier, the holiday company that her father worked for so proudly had captured her imagination by launching a new advert involving a child and her teddy bear. The tag line at the end was: 'Discover your smile'. Until that point, we hadn't known that she had heard the messages – we just thought she liked the bear. She could never have known how needed her words were.

Fifteen hours earlier, I had sat in the same kitchen on a conference call with the same holiday company and no one was smiling. On 26 June, thirty-eight tourists had been killed when a gunman, affiliated to the terrorist organisation Islamic State, opened fire as they relaxed on the beach in Port El Kantaoui, Sousse, Tunisia. Thirty of those were British and had travelled there with the holiday company and airline TUI. Tom's airline. He had flown several of those holiday-makers out to that beach in the days before.

The call was between civil servants, police, UK DVI, Kenyon and the holiday company to ascertain exactly what had transpired. The purpose of this phone call was to bring the agencies together before the foreign secretary chaired COBR. We were gathering what is called in emergency planning, borrowed from the military of course, 'the SITREP': a situational report that is a picture of what is happening on the ground and what needs to be done next.

There was clear frustration and bewilderment from all participants at the behaviour of government civil servants. TUI was digesting the news that a man with an AK-47 had opened fire on their holidaymakers in Tunisia. The government response initially reminded me of those early days after the Bali bombings, fifteen years earlier. I was listening to a surreal political battle between government departments about how many British citizens had died in the shooting. The civil servants were arguing with the data from TUI and appeared unaware, even dismissive, of how much useful knowledge and insight a modern holiday company would have about its own clients. I was wearing two hats on the call – as an adviser to UK DVI and as a member of a professional group that advised airlines and holiday companies in times of emergency.

Public sector responders are often quite disparaging of the private sector partners in disaster response. I have heard police describe an airline who had lost a craft as 'murderers' and tell them that the only kit they needed to remember to bring was their chequebook. However, ever since that staircase in Bristol, I knew that the 'other side' was often hurting too. Many of the dead from Ground Zero were corporate. After 9/11, chief executives from some of the wealthiest financial companies on the planet sat up every night for months to write condolence notes and plan funerals. To arrange financial packages that exceeded any insurance offer. It is hubris for the public sector to think that they are always purer, superior.

TUI was rapidly receiving almost-exact numbers from their representatives on the beach and at the hotel, between thirty and forty deceased with many more injured. At the resort, the holiday reps had followed their training and corralled the bereaved, who had often been next to or close by their loved ones when they were shot, into an area within the hotel. TUI was desperately trying to argue with the UK Foreign and Commonwealth Office, who was asserting that these numbers were overstated, that there may be only three or four fatalities in total.

This shooting felt visceral and personal to Tom. It was an attack on his passengers and he felt responsible for taking them there in the first place. All holidays in Tunisia were cancelled and TUI activated plans to go and collect the survivors and other holidaymakers. It was time for Tom to go and bring his passengers home.

He was selected to be in the crew for the first of the repatriation flights, one of the 'safe pairs of hands' who could provide the ultimate reassurance to passengers and keep steady control of crew. He was desperate to get it right.

I worked with the company overnight on a briefing that would be read out over the tannoy to the passengers. It was to be read out by the captains, including Tom. Tom and I sat in bed with our laptops open. I emailed TUI crisis management my draft – some words of comfort and explanation that would also prepare the passengers for the next steps. They were important witnesses to a terrorist attack. Before they could go home, sink exhausted into bed or a bath, they would need to be interviewed by counter-terror police in the UK. The airline made sure that somebody got them a cup of tea first but couldn't guarantee the nature or manner of the police interview experience. We had no idea what mental or physical state the passengers boarding the planes would be in. I was mindful of the many stories from families of the 2004 tsunami about making their way onto flights still soaking wet and bleeding from cuts and gashes. When they got back to the UK, they realised they had neither car keys nor house keys as all had been lost in the swirling waters. Councils rang around to pass this information on to each other and for the later flights they had locksmiths at the ready at the airport to help people get into their houses. So TUI was ready in case survivors' personal effects were still being held as part of the crime scene and they needed to help their passengers access their homes.

A few minutes later, my words pinged into Tom's inbox as a script, in an email from his management team.

The deceased would be under the care of the Tunisian authorities but with interest from all of the world's counter-terror agencies, and British detectives joined a queue of their international comrades for access to evidence and briefings. We knew we would want to check the identifications again once the bodies were in the care of a UK coroner.

We arranged a quiet civilian repatriation process and everything was in place for UK DVI to take charge of the deceased. Then, just as it was supposed to get underway, I heard the *Today* radio programme question this decision. I listened in horror as John Humphrys suggested that if David Cameron really cared about the British dead, they would be repatriated with full military honours. My phone rang minutes later; it was the new UK DVI co-ordinator and we watched together as all of her carefully laid plans unravelled. The government wanted this to look powerful and impressive and this time the ceremony went ahead.

We had reasons to worry. Initial reports had contained concerning warning signs. Some of the dead had been visually identified, followed up by checking using passport photos. But several of the dead were physiologically similar and wearing similar beachwear. Their next of kin, who could have provided the ante-mortem information, had sometimes died next to them. At the later inquest, one survivor recounted looking through multiple photographs of the deceased, shown to her by Tunisian police. She could not be sure that any of them were her missing friend. She then spotted the glitter toenail polish that her friend was wearing and was taken to see that body and did then confirm the identity.

Politicians growled that this was a counter-terror incident, 'not DVI', which is completely at odds with my view that the two processes should be run together and are complementary. But the new UK DVI co-ordinator, our first female co-ordinator, battled to be able to run additional checks. A team was assembled in Westminster to open each of the coffins and confirm the identities of the deceased. But this was only after the families had each greeted 'their' coffin. The time it took for confirmation was excruciating. We bit our nails during the wait and rehearsed the conversations we would have to have with the bereaved if we were wrong. Fortunately, on this occasion, all the identifications were correct.

The government response was chaotic but TUI had detailed plans, staff volunteers trained to be a response team and a Kenyon contract that meant that hopefully the families saw little of that. Later, I saw a government debrief report that would describe this incident as 'quiet' – emphasising how little the government had had to do. They didn't seem to realise that the job list had been as big and as overwhelming as it always is with these sorts of events, it had just been completed by someone else.

Tom brought his share of the survivors and the bereaved home. Later, a number of families even took the time to write to TUI to thank them for what they had done in the resorts and on the flight. But even now, I think he blames himself for taking those holidaymakers to the beach. And wonders if he did enough for their families when he brought them home. He felt a form of survivor guilt that is common among those who play some part as a link in a disaster's chain of events and then observe the incident's effects at a distance. When he returned home that night he was weary, smelling of 'plane' – that heady mix of sweat, plastic containers of reheated food, urine, metal and a miasma of fuel vapours – but wanted to talk.

When he had printed off the tannoy script and put it into his bag, he said, it had seemed insignificant, no tool for a task as big as this. But then when he read it out, he saw not just the passengers but also his crew visibly relax and ready themselves. He understood now that at a family's worst time, these little things could make a difference. Tom had finally got to see what I did. What the advice did. And why some of my nights had been so very late. He suddenly understood why sometimes I had shut the door on him and the children, arrived late to the meal, sat in the car outside a party. We only had one chance to get this right.

The central government response to the Tunisia disaster, for me, sounded the death knell for the 2000s era of disaster planning. Something had been lost from its heart, but ultimately it was a slow rot that had been setting in for years, since one of the biggest emergency planning operations in UK history: the 2012 Olympic Games.

For the first decade of the century, our entire planning community had focused on readying for what could go wrong at the Olympics. It had been one of the many legacies of the terrible events of 7 July 2005:

on the same day that Tessa Jowell, David Beckham and London Mayor Ken Livingstone were in Singapore celebrating winning the bid to host the games, news had reached them that their citizens back home were being ripped apart across our capital's transport network. This brutal awakening meant they took planning for the Olympics seriously. There was no need to convince Tessa Jowell of what she might face if a disaster occurred at the opening ceremony.

Private and public sector planners, airlines, local government, hospitals and military all had an interest. Emergency planners all around had been co-opted cheerfully into the planning and, although we had a full and terrifying list of things that could go wrong (including a bomb at the opening ceremony, a mass stabbing in the Olympic park, Clostridium difficile or syphilis outbreak in the athletes' village),[45] ultimately we too were infected by the spirit of the games. We were working on something chirpy for a change, with singing and volleyball and dressage and purple track-suited volunteers. People willingly signed up for twenty-four-hour rosters from the spring of 2012 onwards and all summer leave was cancelled. Preparing for the games seemed to infuse society with a number of little tweaks and touches that just made the United Kingdom a nicer place to be for one summer. More united.

However, by the time of the actual games, there was a new government in charge and their intentions seemed a little different. I was used to attending meetings where we planned for the logistics of post-disaster. I expected to plan for the survivor reception centres and for crowd management. But there was something different about the Home Office meetings just before the Olympics. As well as the practical resources, some civil servants also wanted to look at how we could 'nudge' the world into responding emotionally to any disaster that might befall the Olympics. Specifically, to keep calm and carry on, attend the 10,000-metre final. The dead should be mourned, with their photos on a t-shirt, but the games would not stop.

'We want it like the Grand National,' said one civil servant. 'Big fences around the dead and dying horses, but the race goes on.'

By the time the shooting in Port El Kantaoui happened, these twinges of unease had hardened into something stronger. The hidden world of emergency planning was an easy target for cuts under the new coalition government and its policy of public-sector austerity. Unless they need it, the public rarely know that it is there so they don't miss it when it is being chipped away. At least, not until something goes wrong. Our training was becoming less and less frequent. Kit was not being replaced and the national mortuary, used to such powerful effect in 2005, was being dismantled piece by piece. In 2018, it would be offered out to local councils in a bizarre jumble sale. Sinks, body storage units, piping and bottles of chemicals up for grabs. Local police forces and councils were told to use a 'Blue Peter' arrangement in the event of a disaster – tacking on marquees and refrigerated units to local hospitals. Stretching and borrowing if an emergency was to occur in their area. The team based with the Home Office and tasked with planning for large numbers of deaths from a chronic event like pandemics, disease and heatwave was slowly wound down. The government stopped funding the DVI courses in Dundee.

By now, the Cabinet Office Emergency Planning College's income was almost entirely generated from the governments of the Middle East, particularly Abu Dhabi and Saudi Arabia. I would be asked to write the courses on mass fatalities planning, care of people and community recovery but would not be welcome to deliver them. Even when the courses were delivered in the UK, the Arabian delegates insisted on male trainers.

To accommodate these courses the college needed more classrooms so they closed down our planners' library. In the process, they also threw out one hundred years of reports that only existed in hard copy, not on any server cloud. Books of survivors' poetry and photographs of children's art exhibitions to remember their lost. Floor plans for the 7 July assistance centre. I was devastated by this, knowing that the best disaster responses are often at the most local level and produce the most fragile of artefacts. This was one area where I could fight back. For years, I had been building my own library and as colleagues retired, they passed on their own hoard of books and reports. The college's librarian rescued as much as he could from the skip before he too retired and, in one last act of rebellion, posted them to me.

Tom, with weary acceptance, put up more shelves.

New guidance was littered with military and management consultancy terminology. In a new world that saw the public sector as sluggish and leftie, we 'humanitarians' with our amateurish, pro bono ways had little traction. Nowhere was this more obvious than the treatment of Disaster Action. Many of the *madres* were in their fifties when they started and so by now had reached their seventies and eighties. Several of their number had been seriously ill or had lost their own fights with illness in the years before. Some of the newest civil servants treated them terribly. Closed them down when speaking at meetings, mispronounced their child's name, disinvited them to events. We were told to take the Disaster Action support leaflets, designed to help the families enquire and demand better treatment, out of the packs that we provided in assistance centres.

The focus had shifted from genuine interest in public perception and resilience in the face of emergencies to 'optics'. Instead of being asked about what we thought survivors might need in any given scenario or how a public health message might be received, we were now being asked to judge whether we thought the prime minister would be able to weather the storm or have to resign. It felt inauthentic and contrived.

More and more frequently, the 'disasterologists', if used at all, would be placed alongside the behavioural insight teams that were proliferating all over UK government. Originally, the risks (things like extreme weather and 'accidental' bridge collapses) and the threats (bad men, terrorism) that had a high likelihood of happening in the next five years were scored and organised into a matrix so we could create a hierarchy of potential damage. But in the later 2000s, this focus shifted to us being asked to provide a score for 'public outrage'. We produced additional papers and reports on this, based on new evidence and case studies. More and more ways to predict and later to 'nudge' human behaviour in emergencies were explored.

There was also strong resistance if I tried to layer the consequences of the disaster onto other societal realities – what I call domino consequences. Disasters don't happen in societal isolation. It would be highly relevant if an area trialling the new Universal Credit welfare benefits system was then hit by a devastating flood, for example. Or if a pandemic occurred at the same time as Brexit negotiations and bad weather.[46] But they liked their plans neat, one risk at a time, so government had no time for the dominoes.

I also had growing concerns about human slavery and trafficking, which is the fastest growing and most lucrative of all global crimes. Everything seemed geared to a certain type of disaster victim, or perhaps, more accurately, a certain type of voter. I was worried that the 'wrong' sort of people would fall off the edge of the plans – the poor, the trafficked, the vulnerable.

According to the new plans, the public would always support the government and its response. They would do just what they were told with the right nudge. But I don't expect, or want, adherence. In fact, over many years I have learned that sometimes I really like it when the plan goes astray and people act out in the aftermath. The whiffs of rebellion often give me reasons to smile and to hope. The braziers in Wavertree burning copies of *The Sun*. Me and the taxi driver stopping for everyone we could on 7/7 in breach of several conditions of his licence. The residents in the Doncaster leisure centre who made Prince Charles go back outside and put plastic overshoes over his brogues in case he walked flood-mud into their living space.

I wasn't looking for coalescence and group think. I was looking for messy, authentic, complicated human responses. I was an emergency planner who did not always believe in the plan.

13
The Script

The plant rooms of the run-down power station were thick with the noise of several hundred excited students. Some were studying 'public service' programmes at nearby colleges; others had travelled from all over the country from theatre make-up courses. Packed into minibuses before breakfast, they now sucked on Capri-Sun cartons and chewed gum. Half of them would soon collect their 'character' and pull on torn clothing and perfect their limps. Others would spend the day using putty and gloss to paint vivid red scars and open fractures, shards of bone sticking out, on their fellow scholars' legs. Clangs of shutting metal doors cut across their shrieks of excitement at their fake injuries. This was Exercise Unified Response, March 2016, the most ambitious disaster exercise ever attempted in the UK.

Just like children in nursery school set up imaginary shops and pretend kitchens, we disaster specialists practise for disaster. In fact, playing pretend disasters is the way that we spend most of our time and might be the only action some see for years.

Depending on the available resources, events may be ambitious and months in the planning with hundreds of extras, make-up, fake blood and costumes – a bit like historical re-enactments or war-games. Sometimes there is simulation technology or virtual reality equipment. Or, at other times, they are what we call 'table top', where we all just pretend that something has happened and then discuss it, like actors reading through a script. To be honest, all versions can feel very silly. They test how our disaster plans will hold up and give everyone – the blue light responders, the advisers, the civil service – the chance to practise making decisions and taking action. The only people who aren't there are the public, who will need to experience the consequences of the decisions for the first time when it actually happens. These exercises are also designed be a display of preparedness and strength and they are usually given impressive-sounding names, often in Latin, which are an endless source of amusement for me – Exercise Brassica was a highlight.

Sometimes we do them at no notice, like a fire alarm, to try out the processes for real. If you're doing this sort of disaster exercise you have to start the 'activation' (usually a phone call) with the words 'Exercise, exercise, exercise'. Then everyone understands and enters into the game with the person at the other end of the phone, like with a toddler pretending to sip the tea. But people can forget to say the code word. I have known hospital emergency planners who have activated an entire helicopter response team and a blood bank delivery by mistake. When I was working at Kenyon, I once picked up the phone to a major African airline who informed me gravely that our full response would be needed to an all-fatal crash near Nairobi and travelling on the flight had been all of the Spice Girls and Elton John. A showbiz massacre! I ran breathlessly up to Alan to inform them that this was BIG. 'Just ring them back,' he counselled calmly, 'and check if there was something they should have said at the start of the call.' To the relief of pop fans everywhere, it was an exercise.

It is a popular policing trick to include celebrities to liven up scenarios but I never put them in myself – too likely to cause confusion. I write a really very good disaster scenario, mainly due to many years of watching *Brookside*, the gritty soap opera set in my hometown of Liverpool in the 1980s. (The show loved a disaster – one storyline involved a helicopter crashing into a house in lockdown due to plague, while one of the characters was mid-seduction.)

My very first major exercise was one year after the 9/11 terrorist attacks of 2001. A full scale, ambitious script involving several counties in the south of England. The crash of a jumbo airliner. We activated a full disaster mortuary, all the kit, hundreds of people, in a series of military buildings in Hampshire. It was a memorable experience. For one thing, I was slightly alarmed by the presence of a group of very well-meaning locals who had volunteered to play the dead. This is a phenomenon that I have encountered several times since and always freaks me out. There is something fundamentally wrong about someone dressed in their swimwear helping you zip them into a body bag. And then, in what would be the first of many times as the new girl, I was pranked by my disaster colleagues. I was told that to give further protection from contamination you wore your white forensic suits without clothes underneath, stark naked. You don't. I spent a number of hours wandering around the exercise, perfectly transparent. To this day, some colleagues will recount the tale at major international conferences. It has often been remarked upon in recent years how much I seem to have been embraced by certain aspects of the forensic community, as a non-ologist. Other disaster planners express surprise that I am always greeted with big hugs and a cheery tale by the crime scene investigators and the mortuary teams. I would like to say that it is because they recognise my insight, skill and fervour. I think it is much more likely that it's because they have seen my nipples.

So to plan for an exercise, you start with a scenario – a three-counties-wide flood, a motorway pile-up, a terrorist attack – and then design a series of action points, or 'injects', to move the story along a bit. The police, fire and ambulance responders are at their most comfortable exercising the first few hours or days – moving kit and vehicles around. Recovery exercises, covering the later stages, are always harder. Everyone has run out of enthusiasm by then.

Of course, the exercise is different to the reality. People tend to be more bullish in the exercise. The general rule is that no one should leave with egg on their faces, particularly any senior bosses. A recent terrorism exercise I organised involved a room of police tactical support units in full, shiny kit, looking a little like scuba divers. The scenario placed terrorists all around an urban centre, armed with both guns and knives, and was based on real tragedies that have played out in areas like Nairobi, Paris and Mumbai. The police played their parts seriously, they spoke only in gruff shouts and made decisions about 'deploying assets' directly into the 'hot zone' without hesitation. But I knew that in a real terror attack it would feel different; those 'assets' would be men and women who will potentially be shot or blown up in front of you. Men and women with families and made of flesh. And one of the most common themes in disaster inquiries is frustration with delays in sending in help.

Nobody pisses or shits themselves with fear in an exercise but many real survivors do. I caused havoc once at an airline exercise by pointing out we'd made a major error when evacuating the 'survivors'. They had all been neatly processed straight from the scene into a witness interrogation area by counter-terror cops, without even so much as a cup of tea. It was assumed they would be fully clothed and dry. But the kinetic forces acting on our bodies during an explosion or a crash mean our clothes are often ripped off completely. We needed to address basic issues of dignity and decency before we did anything else. Before they could be questioned, the survivors would need clothes and a chance to clean themselves up. A silver blanket wasn't going to do it.

A similar mistake was made for real after the 7/7 bombings. Survivors were hustled out of spaces without their trousers and with urine running down their legs. For a few years, the Met had a stockpile of tracksuits in many sizes. I am not sure if anyone could find them now.

The scenario for Exercise Unified Response was the collapse of an office block onto a busy station during rush hour. It had been two years in development and would last for four days. It involved thousands of people, including representatives from a number of European governments. It cost millions of pounds and had received a large European grant.[47] Responders were allowed to take over Littlebrook power station in Kent, which was due to be demolished. A mock-up of Waterloo tube station had been built and rubble, scaffolding and eight retired tube carriages had been brought in. The BBC beamed some of their *Breakfast* show from within the scene of make-believe carnage. By nightfall, it looked like the set of a Hollywood blockbuster.

Staging all this in a decommissioned power station made perfect sense logistically and also added a horribly realistic dystopian feel of the end of the world. I got to crawl through a tunnel into the scene as sparks from fire fighters' saws flew around me and the students earned their day off by wailing and weeping. Huge amounts of time and effort and resources had gone into building this set and it was brilliantly dangerous, chaotic and claustrophobic. Urban search and rescue teams shouted at each other in the agreed response lexicon.[48] Mannequins were impaled and buried. Water poured out of pretend broken pipes. The 'national evaluators' all met for our briefings and to download our evaluation app on to our mobile phones, frustrated by a rubbish Wi-Fi signal.

However, minimal thought had been given to the welfare of the thousands of 'players' and we were bitterly cold and hungry. It did not stop raining for the entire week. The woeful state of the pitifully small number of portaloos threatened to become a humanitarian incident all of its own. But that wasn't the point. We were not the point. This was going to look good for the cameras; this one was all about the 'optics'.

By now, things appeared to have gone back in time in terms of behaviours and attitudes to disaster planning. The collegiate banter and inclusivity of the mid-2000s was gone. The spaces were filled with big firemen and aggressive policemen. There was no time or tolerance for a woman sent into review the delicate bricolage of their practice but not wearing their uniform. My observations on the 'Mass Fatalities Work Stream' would need to be uploaded, via an app, in as few characters as possible. The deaths of over 300 men, women, children and two newborn babies, the injuring physically and mentally of another 1,000, were to be rendered into 'obs' no longer than a tweet. These 'obs' could be viewed in real time on large screens like a rolling breaking news update. But there was no room for nuance or detail.

For what felt like the fiftieth time, I climbed rusty and dripping iron stairs to attempt another failed download of 'the app'. 'Swipe up, swipe up!' shouted a senior London Fire Brigade commander at me impatiently, leaning over me and my phone in an onslaught of spittle and halitosis. 'Fucking academics,' he muttered as he strode off.

Annoying as it was, the app was not the foremost problem in my mind in this strange artificial space. I had been in denial for eight weeks previously, blaming my missed periods on stress and busy-ness. But then I had bought a test in a late-night Kent petrol station a few days earlier and it confirmed that Tom and I appeared to have made a surprise baby that doctors had warned would kill me. That blue line had made me happy and excited and sad and terrified.

I fought hard to keep all of this out of my head and concentrate on the steel and mud and shouting of the exercise. I had been schooled for many years by the senior female police and fire and ambulance responders that you kept your woman-ness out of your day job. If you needed to throw up you did it discreetly in a bush where no one would see. I learned from detectives who'd had years of fertility treatments or chemotherapy and only a handful of their bosses knew.

One of the main objectives of the exercise was to bring together the Disaster Victim Identification teams from eight countries. We gathered them in their holding area and they stood in geographically organised isolation, eyeing their foreign counterparts with suspicion.

Most teams looked pumped up and excited; there were some high fives and lots of catch-up chat in

Hungarian and German. My eyes were drawn to the French team. They were wearing their very stylish and much-envied black bomber jackets, with 'Police Identification de Victimes' emblazoned on the back. To me, the women carried themselves like Lauren Bacall and the men were straight out of a Givenchy ad. I had met them before and they were usually so cocky and confident but now their eyes were cast down and they were clearly weary. They kept to themselves for the next three days.

It turned out they had come to us almost straight from the Bataclan terrorist attacks in Paris weeks earlier and you could tell.[49] I had heard the first response unit into the Bataclan talk about being 'destabilised' as they entered the scene. They did not mean destabilised metaphorically or emotionally. They were literally pulled over by the hands of dying men and women grabbing at their trouser legs. I smiled at the French team in *solidarité* and they let me take a photo of them in their jackets. Fifteen weeks after we stood together in the Kent rain, the French team would don those jackets again and head to Nice for yet another terrorism deployment.

There was no room allocated on the exercise plan, in the whole of the enormous, redundant power station, for the meeting of the Mass Fatalities Co ordinating Group. This should have been the nerve centre for the key people tasked with caring for the dead. The meetings were delayed while space was found and the formidable coroner was not impressed. It was a bad-tempered start and set the tone for the next few days. The other groups had also forgotten to update her and her mood was darkening with every failed attempt to get information. London Fire's exercise lead arrived to give us all another hearty bollocking about failing to regularly update our 'obs' to the app. He learned a valuable lesson that day about interrupting a hungry, displaced coroner. The straw for the coronial camel's back was the deteriorating state of the portaloos. She had just been walked in on while having a wee, as all the locks were broken.

The exercise mortuary was trialling a number of new ways to get confirmed information on identification out as soon as possible. The advent of social media means that we are now never fast enough with the names of those killed.[50] More and more families were making formal complaints to police forces about finding out via social media that their loved one had died. While we are still removing the bodies from a scene to refrigerated holding spaces, photo collages of the 'possibly dead' are already being constructed by local media and Facebook. Google People Finder and phone applications like 'Find my Friend' mean everyone can be a disaster detective now.[51]

I can always tell which emergency planners have seen the death wrought by disaster and which have only been told about it. It is like being a virgin back in year eleven and only knowing about the carnal act from Mrs Mathison's leaflets while everyone else seems to be at it. The most grizzled disaster responders, my Kenyon mentors, who had probably reached the 10,000 body count mark, wrote the best, most realistic plans. The dangerous, unworkable, traumatising mass fatality plans are written by the virgins. New fast-track civil servants serving a six-month placement at the Home Office, who have never been to a funeral home never mind inside a disaster mortuary, are sometimes asked to draft plans, instead of bringing in specialists like me. They bend and break the processes to speed them up; ignore welfare and rest space for the APTs; forget the storage space for 100 pairs of clogs and a 100 pairs of wellington boots.[52] They have no knowledge of the ways that the disaster fates play their tricks. They have never seen the coincidences that pepper every disaster I have ever seen: two people seated separately on a flight, never met, but with the same name, middle name, surname and date of birth. Two people on the same train, unknown to each other, with identical tattoos of tiger and dragon locked in fighting embrace inked from nape of neck to buttocks. One of their mums filling out the form with an emphasis on the tattoo as a 'unique' identifier – find the tattoo and you will find my boy. Except you won't, necessarily. Instead, if you are not thorough and do not realise that wildly improbable coincidences happen all the time, and the need for DVI, you will send her back a random stranger from seat 13D.

Novice planners also often don't realise that no matter how snazzy the technology is, there is still so much room for error in the disaster mortuary – a knocked over pile of papers here, a mislabelled sample there, an app that won't load. The mortuary at Unified

Response over-relied on a number of portable whiteboards, which was a fatal error. Boobs, buttocks, arms swiped too close and vital lines of text – the locations of the bodies in the bays – were lost.

London Fire Brigade had a number of new mannequins that they wanted to embed into the Exercise Unified Response scene. These included two pregnant mannequins complete with detachable full-term babies. These mannequins represented two women in the scenario who had been in the late stages of pregnancy and the babies that they had delivered as a result of the shock of the incident. Both babies had died but the mothers had not. English law is strict and prescriptive around the 'rights' (or lack of) of the unborn baby in order to protect a woman's right to abortion. Under criminal law, a baby has to have lived and breathed separately from its mother to count as having its own separate personhood. This ambiguity was of great concern to the coroner, as it would impact whether these babies could be considered as 'victims' of the incident and part of the death toll, and their right to a separate inquest. She put a lot of thought into the handling of those babies but the situation became increasingly tense because no one had thought through those details in order to be able to answer her questions. They had just wanted to try out their new toys. Unhelpfully, it was at that point that the responders realised that they couldn't actually find the little vinyl bodies of the fake neonates. They had been lost somewhere in the body holding area. Ironically, this unintentional plot twist felt so real and so awful and so likely all at once.

On the real-time 'obs' board, most of the tweets related to the fact that the MFCG was running horribly behind time according to the script. The coroner was supposed to be chairing and she needed to be brought back on task. She needed to forget about the lost babies. I was dispatched to pass these messages and trudged back across the filthy, sodden site to face the coroner, feeling as though I was off to my own execution. On the walk over, I had to stop and grab onto rough concrete walls several times, doubled over in pain. As I stood in front of her and she bollocked me for mumbling, I was aware that blood had started to seep into the tights I was wearing under my jeans because it was freezing.

I apologised for my incoherence to Her Majesty's coroner and stumbled out of her meeting and into the one vacant portaloo. I feebly held on to the broken lock to keep it in place and looked down at the floor, caked in shit and mud. And there, in that place, the Last of the Titans checked out.

14

The Extra Dove

The new laboratories at the University of Lincoln were state of the art and very shiny. I had been given a position there as a senior lecturer in disaster forensics and the law and I had a long-running joke with the lab receptionist who was responsible for signing in the packages: taking delivery of chemicals for the explosives scholars, frogs and beetles for the biologists, 3D-printed plastic skulls and synthetic blood for the forensic faculty. She and I would joke each morning about a pretend delivery for me: alpacas, a lifetime's supply of Cadbury's Creme Eggs, Chris Hemsworth. One spring morning I got to bring our joke to its zenith – when thirty-five actual vicars in black shirts and dog collars were delivered to reception for the attention of Lucy Easthope.

By the spring of 2017, the team of advisers who support the Archbishop of Canterbury, the most senior clergy in the Church of England, had been meeting with me for over a year. It had begun when a number of clergy who worked alongside police forces in their communities attended my Disaster Victim Identification training. Word spread and it turned out that the Church leadership also wanted to be ready for disaster. Through both a spiritual and a constitutional role, some of the Church of England's bishops sit in the House of Lords, so they need to consider their position on all of society's latest issues. And like other members of the House of Lords, they scrutinise legislation and act as an independent voice. They wanted to be better informed about what we could be facing.

Their theology meant that they were well placed to understand the role that resting remains and settled graves play in society. We talked extensively about the ethics of the constant re-testing of the remains, the torturing of the dust after 9/11 and how a middle ground seemed to have been found in Lac-Mégantic, Québec, and the labs of Montreal. We found ourselves focusing very hard on that particular aspect of disaster recovery: how we should protect and gather, then test and return remains. They could see that how identification science and particularly DNA testing should be treated in a disaster had the potential to be as big an issue as organ donation or debates around human fertility and embryology, all of which are regularly taken to the House of Lords.

'It strikes me,' said the chair at the end of one meeting, 'that this is a much bigger issue than I realised when Lucy first made her way to us.' Then he said something that sounded like a line out of a movie version of the story of Robin Hood or Henry VIII: 'The bishops must be told.'

We decided to team up and organise a wider

discussion on Disaster Victim Identification and specifically the link between the care of the bereaved and deceased and the longer-term recovery of communities. The Church of England's policy team were particularly interested in the forensic aspects of recovering the remains and identifying them.

I planned to bring together the theologians, the scientists, the police and the coroners for a full day's event that I hoped might be as galvanising as the effects of the tsunami and Lord Clarke's report had been in the early 2000s. I had ideas for funding and new training programmes, more imagination and more curveballs. Perhaps the DVI courses at Dundee could be re-started again? Police and anthros would co-train, not just for the scientific aspects of identification but for all the challenges that would come with communicating the work to families.

We were due to gather at the Church of England's headquarters, Church House, which is near the Cabinet Office's building in Westminster. The date for our meeting was set for 13 June 2017.

As the day approached, I was more nervous than I could remember ever being. This felt like the culmination of twenty years of work. Looking back, I was also trying to ignore the fact that I wasn't feeling at all well. I had spent the weekend in Ireland at the joyous wedding of a childhood friend and on the flight back started to feel extremely nauseous. I put it down to travel sickness but had a sense that something deeper might be amiss. I just didn't have the luxury of paying attention to what that something might be.

My mouth was dry as I tried to condense every lesson I had absorbed from every disaster I had seen into a thirty-minute opening pitch. I then presented the audience with a specific disaster scenario. This scenario was the sum of all my fears and I wanted to persuade people that we needed to be ready for it. The scenario was made up of multiple factors, with each one making the recovery ten times harder.

The scenario involved homes and the destruction of 'the furniture of self'. Some personal effects would be destroyed, some only damaged – and these would need to be picked through by a specially hired contractor over several months before being returned in the brown boxes that I had shopped for at Kenyon. The vital tools for the ante-mortem part of the process, the toothbrushes, the passports, would be gone too.

It would be a tower block and there would be concerns over the actions of local authorities and building enforcement agencies, gas safety sign-off. And the residents of the tower would be from diverse backgrounds. I wanted to make the point that our scenarios and exercises were overwhelmingly built to accommodate a very specific type of white Briton with surnames like Smith or Philips, who would need no translation of any of the paperwork, and a grieving family who required a nod to some rites and rituals of a lapsed C of E faith. There would be an occasional Ali in the pretend paperwork but no real consideration of the way that faith, religion or culture would affect our practices. For this scenario, I argued, we would need a deployment of really well-trained family liaison officers and, where possible, fast access to DVI-trained interpreters.[53]

The next factor was the really big one. It would involve loss of life, fire and a great deal of 'forensic uncertainty'. There would be cremains and dust. There would be the most complex of DNA challenges: hard-to-access samples and no clear biological kinship and a lengthy, drawn-out identification process. With human slavery and trafficking on the rise, we would also not know who everyone was in the tower. Lost and hidden people might be in there too. This was where I wanted to argue for the most change – support and resources and protection for the national anthropology team and their work. And, crucially, clear guidance on how long to continue DNA testing on remains.

My hopes for the meeting were dashed almost before we began. I think the senior detectives in the room were discombobulated by being part of, rather than leading a discussion and this was not their environment. A training room with psalms etched on the walls was outside of their comfort zone and they shifted uncomfortably in their chairs. One senior delegate, who had arrived late, dismissed the burgeoning DNA discussions, stating that all was in hand with the Human Tissue Authority, the organisation set up in the wake of the Alder Hey inquiry. 'Forgive me, sir,' I challenged, 'but actually I have a letter here from the HTA. They do consider this a gap in the legislation and they would welcome an official position.' The meeting went downhill from there.

The strongest ire was reserved for the final factor in

my scenario. All of the national guidance was predicated on collaboration after disaster, that local agencies and communities would muddle together against a common enemy. Local government were generally the ones in charge of the 'recovery' after a disaster but my question was, what if the local government were also somehow to blame for the disaster? What then? Who would have the moral authority and the technical legitimacy to manage the families and their mass grave? I referenced the hurt caused to generations of Scouse families by Hillsborough.

'We will never see another Hillsborough,' said one attendee, 'and we can't plan on a fantasy.'

Others were more supportive. The human rights lawyer who specialised in the care of the deceased body spoke passionately, challenging the paternalism of the decision-making being done behind closed doors. The scientists talked about the implications of dwindling resources and the privatisation of forensic laboratories. Dave, the DVI detective I'd worked with on the downing of MH17 in Ukraine and my cheery nemesis, took me most by surprise. I was touched that he had even made it to the meeting, fitting it in after a deployment to the suicide bombing at a pop concert in Manchester Arena twenty-two days earlier. In the days before, he and I had conducted several calls late into the night about the personal effects contract that would be drafted for that response. For the handbags and the tubes of cherry flavoured lip balm and lots and lots of shoes that were lost as people fled.

'There is something here that needs looking at,'

Dave said, defiantly. I smiled weakly at him with gratitude.

Lucina Hackman was there too. As well as being the curator of pre-natal bones at the University of Dundee, she is the country's leading anthropologist for the recovery of remains found at fire scenes and explosions. After lunch, she ploughed through an impressive presentation on how to protect and triage the scene of a high-temperature fire in a domestic setting. We had become too focused on explosions; our new policing protocols were preoccupied with tissue and what was graphically described as 'pink mist' generated by suicide bombings and we needed to think about the way that fire does something different. In a fire, the bodies themselves become their own accelerants – fuel. And at the highest temperatures, human bone takes on the composition of first-fired pottery and even in the safest hands will turn to a fine dust at the tiniest hint of pressure. She showed us how old-school anthropological techniques can provide some of the reassurance of DNA testing without the need for perpetual testing or the destruction of the remains.[54] Many of the techniques she was describing were near-identical to those used in the most delicate of archaeology digs, with grids, callipers and tiny brushes. She wanted to impress on the responders that they would need resources, space and autonomy. And, most importantly, time.

Although it had not gone as well as I hoped, we did get to the end of the day with a set of actions. And we agreed that the scenario would be presented at a further meeting to be held in the House of Lords that summer. As it turned out, that event never made it into anyone's diary.

Towards the end of the day, I stood in the ladies' loos and stared into the mirror at a face that was a bizarre shade of *Simpsons* yellow. Lucina was next to me, washing her hands. She had been a nurse before studying forensics. She looked up at me and said, 'Go to hospital, Lucy. Now.'

When Jay picked me up from my home train station, I asked him to divert to our local A&E. Normally there is a wait of several hours but as soon as my blood results came in I was shown to a bed.

I was still there, awake, when I received the first text message. It said simply, 'Have you seen?'

It was a fire in Flat 16, Grenfell Tower, the Royal Borough of Kensington and Chelsea, London. A tower block of 129 homes. Every safety measure failed and every method in place to contain the spread of the fire collapsed. The tower was a charred wreck.

Later that day, left alone on a hospital bed with a tiny TV screen and my phone, waiting for surgery as the symptoms of acute pancreatitis worsened, I tried to assess what was happening. A Mass Fatalities Co-ordinating Group had been established but all the usual lines of communication were eerily quiet. No word had gone out to the UK DVI teams. The fire now appeared to be under control but the scene was clearly one of utter devastation. There had been other recent fires in tower blocks but a major difference here was the lack of containment. The news footage had moved to showing huddles of the exhausted and traumatised people at the base of the tower and frantic interviews with family members about their missing relatives.

Sitting in my pyjamas, I fired off emails and texts to my colleagues – some were in the thick of responding; some, like Lucina, waiting to be called. Her role would only kick in when the ashes had cooled and there were no more lives to be saved. UK DVI colleagues were agitated. They had heard nothing. Nobody was asking for help.

With every sinew of my ailing body, I wanted this response to go well. I texted colleagues at the Metropolitan police, forensic colleagues, other emergency planners, those of us who had been at the meeting the day before. It felt as if we had somehow rattled the fates too much with my scenario. The theologians later admitted that the coincidence of the similarities between the story we told and the reality had haunted them ever since.

'Get some rest, love,' a healthcare assistant counselled as she brought everyone else their meal. I was nil by mouth. Another nurse told me to unplug my charger 'for health and safety please, love – fire risk'.

Eventually my beloved uncle Mike texted me to shut up. To lie back on the cool pillow and get well. People could die from acute pancreatitis and in his line of work, he should know. I took another dose of liquid morphine and sank back on my aerated mattress. Very briefly, I gave up.

★   ★   ★

The fire that turned Grenfell Tower into a 'burnt matchbox in the sky'[55] is presumed to have been started in or around a fridge-freezer in the kitchen. The fire began just after midnight on 14 June 2017. Grenfell Tower was a 1970s tower block with a basement, a ground floor and then twenty-three further floors. Between 2012 and 2016, it had undergone substantial refurbishment and the safety management of that, and all aspects of the block, is the subject of a long-running public inquiry and what is likely to be some of the most drawn-out corporate litigation and criminal investigation ever seen in the UK. As part of the works, the building had been clad in foam insulation and aluminium composite materials. The types of materials used are now known to have been implicated as enhancing the spread of fire in a number of earlier incidents.[56] Residents were initially advised to 'stay put', even as the fire spread all around them and their flats filled with smoke.

The first deceased recovered from the scene had not burned inside but had jumped or fallen to their deaths. Two further casualties died in hospital. More deceased were dragged outside from the lower floors by police and fire teams, but many others would need to be recovered painstakingly from inside the flats in a process taking fourteen weeks.

Seventy people died that night and in the days afterwards, and a further seventy were injured. In a grim echo of the scenario we had explored in Exercise Unified Response, one woman, heavily pregnant, lost her baby at thirty weeks. He was later added to the list of deceased, his mother exhausted and injured.[57] A woman who died in hospital later was added to the death toll in February 2018, bringing it to seventy-two.

The scenes of disaster that I had become accustomed to by 2017 involved looking down and looking into. Disaster scenes to me were craters, huge cleaved-out furrows made by aircraft noses, the vast expanse of basements under the Twin Towers. But here, at Grenfell Tower, you had to look up. Properly crane your neck and step backwards to take in the immense height of the tower. The blackness of the building, stark against blue sky.

I had asked to walk around the roads at the base of the tower and Tara from the local health commissioning body had reluctantly agreed to take me. 'Come on!' she hissed, with the furtiveness of a cat burglar. 'We can't be too long.' The scene is protected fiercely by the devastated local communities and even now, at the time of writing, outsiders are viewed with great suspicion. But I wanted to try to take in what was here and what was lost before I did anything else. I also wanted to try to understand what it must feel like to live underneath it now.

It was six weeks after the fire. On street corners and lamp posts, handmade posters were placed to remind visitors not to take photographs. It was the first time that I had seen such an edict at the site of a disaster. Metropolitan police teams were well into work on removing the remains and were installing a lift alongside the building. Teams were searching the flats and other spaces and, poignantly, all of the rubbish chutes. Police officers threw plastic bottles down the chutes in an attempt to demonstrate an absence of any bodies. There had been unconfirmed reports from the night of the fire of families trying to throw their babies and young children down the chutes to safety.

On later visits, as summer turned into autumn, the green leaves fell from nearby trees and exposed the dark totem even more starkly. The distress in the children visibly increased at this time. When their teachers and the local mental health workers tried to get to the bottom of why, the older children explained that once they had gone to bed, they would pull their curtains back and watch the silhouettes of police teams working in the tower like shadow puppets. The children would assume that a long torch was a bone, a large bag was a body and were terrifying themselves and each other with tales of the night. When the wind blew, the structure would creak and whistle. For months, thick black dust had blown from the tower onto the homes and cars around it, which was a major source of distress – 'They think it might be, you know … human ash,' mouthed the horrified social workers sent to try to support the families.

I had been invited by responders, from the NHS and from a recovery group set up by ministers, to provide advice on a number of aspects of the recovery process – personal effects, housing and the longer-term strategy. To get to me, local responders had been passed around, from contact to contact, I found out later. When I asked government colleagues why they did not pass on my details there was some fumbling and discussion about not being able to track me down. Eventually, a colleague there said to me, 'Look, it's complicated. It's not your usual disaster – this is a Duggan situation.' He was referring to the rioting in 2011 across a number of London boroughs that occurred when a young man, Mark Duggan, was shot by police. He told me the local community was a 'tinderbox' – which seemed a cruel analogy. The government was afraid of rioting and of losing control of this 'foreign' place. I think they were worried that I might be the one to start it.

North Kensington, in the heart of London, has a brave history of trouble-making for those in power. It is vibrant, diverse and home to one of the largest carnivals in the world in Notting Hill. The area has some of the greatest levels of deprivation in the UK. Grinding child poverty, inadequate housing, low employment. Beginning just two streets away from Grenfell Tower, South Kensington has the greatest concentration of millionaires and some of the most expensive urban dwellings in the world. Tourists flock here, to the shops of Kensington High Street, the Royal palaces, Knightsbridge, the Natural History Museum. Disparity of wealth is everywhere in the UK but the blunt proximity in this place is breathtaking.

The fire in Grenfell Tower occurred at a time of intense political sensitivity. It was one year almost to the day of the Brexit result and British politics was in turmoil. Grenfell Tower was a great big, visible, itching humiliation.

All governments struggle with the embarrassment of a disaster on their patch but against a backdrop of political crisis and uncertainty, it creates intolerable pressure. A disaster at this time makes a government look like it can't keep its own citizens safe, never mind fight a war or negotiate a new era of global diplomacy. So, they tried to play Grenfell down. When international offers of help, of specialist search and rescue and scanning equipment came in they were batted away. Nothing to see here. After the fire, the Metropolitan police had also immediately declined additional support from the UK Disaster Victim Identification team and the national anthropological response team.

The initial death toll was estimated at well over two hundred souls. Lists of residents were out of date, incomplete and took no account for visitors. It was also the religious festival of Ramadan. On that warm June day, darkness did not fall until about 10 p.m., so one fear was that many Muslims would have been visiting relatives in the tower to break the fast. In the weeks after the fire, posters of missing persons were taped to lamp posts and placed on boards in the local sports centre. Most of the dead were found in twenty-three flats and the scene was perilous and spread over multiple floors of an unstable structure. The fire had been intensely destructive and the remains were fragile and often 'co-mingled'. In one case, eleven deceased were found closely entwined. Something approaching a final death toll took months to emerge.

'Gold Command' for 'Grenfell Recovery' was

housed in a central London office block. Secure lifts sent by your hosts spilled you out onto the correct floor. To my jaded and tired eyes it was as if all the worst bit of disaster planning in the second decade of the twenty-first century had been crammed together. It was full of consultants and hastily procured advisers. The office kitchen fridges were packed with cans of Coca Cola and energy drinks. The energy felt like *The Apprentice* – lots of pitching ideas and striding purposefully but there was no Disaster Action here and little room for heart. The few colleagues that I did recognise from other times looked wary and weary.

There was no community invited into the shiny office block, only responders. Residents were corralled into other spaces, newly procured community centres that smelt of fresh paint. Central government promoted a number of messages within the local North Kensington community, in media interviews and public meetings. That this was terrible, that they were very, very sorry. That disaster and mass death was a new phenomenon and the last time ministers had seen anything a bit like this was Hillsborough in 1989. This was unique, unprecedented and could never have been foreseen. And that there were very few plans or policies in the UK for this sort of event.

The tower had taken everything from its surviving residents. They had lost loved ones. They lost their home. They lost their personal effects. They lost their children's innocence and at times it felt like they had lost their sanity. They lost the fragile trust they had had in the state. And, like the people of Aberfan, they were left full of *hiraeth* – the longing for a place to which there was no return.

A group of bereaved and survivors had formed an advocacy and support organisation, Grenfell United. They had their diaries filled with every possible consultation and a conveyor belt of public meetings. They were asked their views on housing policies. On funding. On the types of seating the bereaved might like to sit on. There was visit after visit to potential office spaces that the council was willing to rent for them. Much of this was well-intentioned but a more cynical view could be that it also kept them very busy at a time when they needed to be girding their loins for a fight for some sort of justice.

Communication around the identification of the deceased was a major issue. Ideally, for the numbers of missing people involved, about 400 police family liaison officers trained in disaster victim identification were needed. But there was nowhere near enough and that left an insurmountable vacuum.[50] The local authority hastily procured social workers to fill the gap, none of whom had ever been trained in family assistance or the identification techniques used after disaster. Almost all of the bereaved spoke languages other than English but the DVI meetings were always in English. Translators were provided and there were Interpol forms in Arabic but no additional supportive leaflets or links to a glossary, and some of the terminology was unfamiliar to even the most experienced translators. Mistakes and misunderstanding about what the process was able to do were perpetuated.

The naming of the dead was problematic from the outset – there were almost no ante-mortem 'exhibits' to collect and from the higher floors only the most fragmented of cremains. I was concerned that there didn't seem to be a strong anthropologist presence at the site itself. The Met took over most of the scene work, sending remains that were bigger than 6mm by 6mm in size to Westminster mortuary, where two anthropologists on commercial contracts set to work analysing them. Everything smaller was put into bags.

For a few weeks in the summer of 2017 it seemed like we might be edging towards the approach seen at Lac-Mégantic. Taking the best of 9/11 but with pragmatism and an end point, with a proper space for this work to be done. A space that the families could perhaps have visited.

I eagerly supplied my notes to the Mass Fatalities Co-ordinating Group, emailing over copies of the DNA policies I had collected from around the world and, most importantly, the Lac-Mégantic forensic strategy that had placed such emphasis on the resting remains.

The Home Office was interested and chose to fly in scientists from the New York laboratories. They advised on the design and requirements of a special facility that could provide the assurance that everyone had been recovered. I waited for a flurry of announcements and for a programme of work. A DNA strategy closely aligned to a forensic anthropology strategy. But the scientists were flown back again and the facility was never built.

Finally, as the community became more and more agitated by the delay, the investigators resorted to secondary identifiers. CCTV of those going into the building in the last week was matched against those coming out. Witness statements were taken from food delivery workers. And, in the end, the list of seventy-two names came from the communities who had lost their people. From the families themselves and from their religious leaders and their GPs, from the North Kensington Law Centre, which had been kept busy for years before the fire with housing disputes and obtaining asylum for victims of torture. There was to be no further attempt to identify remains and the DVI aspects of the incident were declared closed.[59]

But what if there is no one to give your name? The list of dead at Grenfell only works if we knew every single person in that building. What if some of Grenfell's residents were hidden and have stayed unaccounted for? Even just one or two. For those who had little record in life, we would be abandoning them to being almost nothing in death, just dust.

On the first anniversary of the Grenfell disaster, seventy-two doves were released at the base of the tower by the bereaved and survivors. To remember the dead in the tower. But then an extra dove was released 'for the unknown'. Many community documents will always write 'at least 72 died'. And in the tunnels under the Westway and on the hoardings around the tower, graffiti art openly questions the death toll. 'Do the maths,' it says.

I have asked members of local advocacy groups a number of times about that extra dove. Initially, I could not understand why it did not signal more community action around the death data. Some community members said they felt like they were made 'to do a deal'. It had, a few whispered, been made clear to them that if they pressed too hard on questions about any unidentified and unofficial residents they would lose national goodwill. That they would be characterised as a slum full of illegal migrants. But local people assert their distrust of their official death toll in quiet ways.

Just as I had feared, we stumbled constantly around issues of culture and race and faith. Records from the night itself show the police call handlers struggling to correctly record and spell Islamic names. Those who died originated from multiple nations including Afghanistan, Italy, Lebanon, Syria, Sudan, Egypt and Eritrea, and more than half of the adult victims arrived in Britain after 1990, some only in the months before the fire. This meant that many of the families of the dead had little knowledge of the UK's long, fractious history with these types of incidents and many appeared to accept the assertions that this was the first time these events had happened. They trusted in certain aspects of the process. When I met with them, they believed that the very latest DNA science had been used here to make sure that every last piece of their loved one had been recovered. That their loved ones could not possibly be in the ash and rubble still held from the site. I have attended many meetings where this has been asserted, over and over, as a comfort.

It has been confirmed that a small number of larger bones remain separately in the care of the Westminster mortuary. There is no clear plan for how they will be allowed to rest. And what about the tiny fragments, the ones under 6mm, co-mingling with a shred of fabric or carpet and the cladding that had accelerated their demise? The dust, and these cremains, were placed into asbestos waste bags. These were wrapped in three further layers of plastic, placed in shipping containers and left on the site that the Met used for large vehicles caught up in complex collision. No sign or marker, and no plan, yet.

What value do we place on these bags of dust? Those shipping containers feature in my dreams now and slowly these remains get written out of the narrative. The sanitisation of the story of the remains and the promulgation of myth of the certainty of the recovery operation is now an insurmountable problem for the recovery of the people of Grenfell. There is nothing new about disputed death tolls; they have always been rounded up or down, points of fierce contention in communities for centuries.[60] But even if that list is as accurate as it can be, I will always have my concerns that we didn't do enough for the remains or the families. Which was ironic, as I had planned and worried that the problem would be that we would do too much.

As time went on, I was asked to advise in more and more areas to do with Grenfell – the team advising the prime minister on the future of the tower, the local health commissioning group, organisations supporting mental health on the ground and the Royal Borough of Kensington and Chelsea, the council. They were the embodiment of the nightmare scenario: a local government organisation already condemned as being a perpetrator left in charge of also 'recovering' the local people.[61] I had assumed that some sort of commissioning group would take over but instead the responsibilities were handed back to the same departments that the bereaved families and the communities blamed. It created the most unhealthy of dependencies – the people you were most angry with held all the keys to the cupboard and all of the financial instruments.

Everything the council did was set against a 200-mile-per-hour headwind of stinging opposition. Nothing landed well. Public meetings would last for four hours. Every meeting, then and now, at the time of writing, would begin with seventy-two seconds of silence and then the shouting would start. Staff would sit and take it, adding it to their own guilt that they had not done more. I ran training sessions on 'good things to try in disaster recovery' for the council and half of the room would sit and weep. One of the hardest sessions was with the small team of occupational therapists who had worked with some of the residents in the tower when they had first moved in. Among the criticisms of responders on the night of the fire was their failure to evacuate vulnerable and disabled residents, who then perished in their flats. These therapists knew every one personally and had helped them get adjustments to their bathroom, handles by their bed. They were haunted that they had helped them live there. Just like Tom with his irrational, toxic guilt that if only he had not flown the plane to Tunisia his passengers would have never been there. I listened, tried to stand them up tall and then sent them back out again.

Council workers took off their lanyards and identity badges on the bus so that people would not know where they worked. All work nights out were cancelled and still are. The national narrative was that they had done nothing on the night itself. Actually, almost 400 workers from the council had attended the scene and the centres around in the first night and day. But because of the anger towards the council, the police had advised them to pretend to be from the Red Cross.

Responders took the greatest comfort from the stories of other places. They visibly relaxed when I told them about other disasters and how the healing process had slowly worked there. They wanted to hear about their setbacks and their little wins. I took to ending the sessions with the Lac-Mégantic 'Happy' video to at least attempt to lighten the mood at the end of very hard days.

From the outside, it looked like the council in particular just kept failing but from the inside, the scale of their task was Herculean. It was the biggest re-housing operation the country had seen on UK soil since the Second World War; new houses had to be found in one of the most expensive places to acquire property in the world. I made a plea to find a way to keep the community together, even musing on whether there would be a way to build something like in Toll Bar, with mobile lodges and a laundry and street signs, in one of the many proximate Royal parks.[62] But a trailer park would not work for the 'optics'. And the council needed to be made to pay up, over and over again. They would be directed to use their surplus to buy up the most expensive flats that they could find in all different parts of the capital. There was a nagging concern in my mind by now that it would be easier in the long run for the police, for local government, if the community was broken up. The trailer park idea may have been a bust but I still feel immense frustration that more could not have been done to preserve some of those physical lifescapes – the connections between place and space and persons that matter more than anything else after disaster.

I was also concerned about the approach taken towards young children and adolescents of the disaster, some of whom were being given formal diagnoses of post-traumatic stress disorder (PTSD).[63] Their anger, expressed through shouting at a teacher or slamming a bedroom door, was taken as something that should be labelled, medicated and then therapised away. But disaster children have every right to be angry. PTSD is a huge diagnosis and is not the same as a situational reaction to trauma that may be treatable and supported. I felt we had to strike a balance and also provide opportunities for advocacy, mentoring and most of all enhancing life chances through education, access to employment and sport. I tried to explain that I had met children of earlier disasters who had accessed periods of mental health support in their teens that had then been recorded and treated as major mental illness. This was something we should be watchful for as it had sometimes counted against the children when they had gone, later in life, for specialist positions in medicine, aviation and the military. One responder in the room said loudly that wasn't an issue here. 'Those were not the sorts of jobs these children would go on to do.'

One obvious and painful reason that the community stayed in a recovery limbo, alongside a quest for justice, was that the place of the fire, their grave, stayed unrested. Grenfell is an above-ground crime scene that is so high it has to have beacon lights attached to it to warn helicopters of its presence. It was not just the local children who were distressed by it, looking out of their bedroom windows at night. People in the surrounding buildings took to drawing their curtains on it and I noticed most would look down at the ground as they passed. Some from neighbouring roads asked to be moved away from it, alongside the surviving families from the tower. Eventually, a decision was taken to cover the blackened shell in material that was frequently referred to in meeting minutes as a shroud.

What remains of the tower has stayed put, for now. The relationship between the tower and the people is complicated – it is a grave, a sacred, hallowed space and a terrible reminder of what was lost. But it is also the chance to dissent. Civil servants and structural engineers feel it would be best for the tower to be demolished for safety. But the communities lobbied that only they would decide when it came down. This was not something to be tidied away. It was a protest by people who had fought gentrification and eviction for years and now they had a chance to leverage some new-found power over those who had controlled them. As a show of strength, of dissent and rebellion, the tower, for now, would agitate, even while its presence is so toxic and so distressing. While it is there, the disaster cannot be moved into history, archived, memorialised. It is a rebellion against the most common behaviour of all in disaster response – the act of forgetting.

At the time of writing, the final fate of the tower is still undecided but my instinct tells me it won't be there for much longer. I fear that the path to some form of 'recovering', particularly for the children, will be hard with it still in its present condition.

The peace that I had briefly observed in Lac-Mégantic seems so very far away.

15

White Chrysanthemums

When the text message beeped, it woke me up. It was well past 8 a.m., which was late for us. Tom and I had sat up into the night talking, first in a corner in the hotel bar and then in the hotel room that family had bought for our anniversary to try to cheer us up.

Tom wasn't well. In recent months, he had developed deafness and tinnitus and kept losing his balance. We had spent the summer going back and forth to specialists and, while we got to the bottom of the diagnosis, he could not fly. It wasn't getting any better and often he would need to sleep all day. I would shush the children around him and they learned to watch CBeebies in silence, with the subtitles on. Scans of his big, bald, handsome head had revealed no tumour in his brain or his sinuses so now we were waiting for the next referral. If he lost his health, his licence would immediately follow. It was becoming clear to him that, at forty-one, he might never fly again.

As well as watching his physical health decline, catching him as he stumbled at a supermarket checkout, learning to speak slower and more clearly, I could see he was being eaten from the inside by all of this. I was jealous of how much the loss of the relationship with his jet was grieving him. I wanted me and the girls to be enough for him. But I knew that without flying, he was not sure what he was.

But Beth, the sender of the text message, also needed urgent attention. I delayed our slot for breakfast and made my call to her. After Grenfell, Disaster Victim Identification training had shrunk back into police forces and there was no money for exercises or more expansive training. The national mortuary had been disbanded and the kit given away in the jumble sale. But I still ran my training courses and I still took calls and provided support and tactical advice.

Beth told me that earlier that night, the bodies of thirty-nine young men and women had been found in the back of a lorry trailer parked up on an industrial estate in Grays, Essex. The driver was under arrest and the police were arranging to move the lorry, with the bodies still inside, to a warehouse. Beth was a local emergency planner and under the terms of the Civil Contingencies Act, she was now responsible for some of what was going to happen next. While the police examined the bodies for both evidence of identity and evidence of crime, Beth was responsible for thinking ahead to the way the local community would react and what the families of the deceased would need.

'I can't believe it, Lucy, I can't believe it. We literally just . . . we just . . .' Beth could barely get her words out. I already knew that part of Essex well. I had been going back and forth from this large town that summer as they had hired me to train and exercise for the most likely scenarios in their area. Beth ran a team of just two other people but had support from other managers at the council and I had been training and working with them for a number of years.[64]

Training there sometimes felt like being a ghost in a strange in-between place. I stayed overnight in a Travelodge full of families on the council's homeless register. On a recent visit, I'd overheard that the family at the next table to me had lost everything in a fire. They had vouchers to spend on meals and I listened in as they worked out how many they had left and tried to quieten their children in the soulless diner. In the evenings, I took to eating in the nearby Lakeside shopping centre as dusk fell. The place felt bleak and deserted, the bright shopfronts blinking to no one. On one occasion, I was pushed out of the way as panting security guards chased a suspected shoplifter from a handbag store. I assuaged my mum-guilt for being away with purchases of neon pink Hatchimals in their artificial shells and farm animals for our growing plastic menagerie back at home.

The only premises that were busy was a mini tuition centre – where little children, heads wrapped in headphones, were learning English and improving their maths in the evenings. The shopfront was glass and I could see the children sat in their booths, concentrating hard. As their parents waited to collect them, I could hear chatter in Arabic and Swahili. To them, England was a stepping stone to a better life, one that they could unlock by learning English. One night, I picked

noodles and sweet and sour chicken in a carton for
my tea and watched a mum and her children share
their chicken nuggets next to me. Under the table, I
could see the backs of their shoes had been cut out to
allow for growing feet because school shoes are
expensive. I knew what my dad would do if he spotted
a family in that situation. He would have tried to pass
the mum any spare money that he could not afford to
give away across the two tables. But these are different
times. I didn't want to offend her. I ate and cleared my
table and moved on.

Beth and I had talked often that summer about her
particular fears in terms of local risks and unrealised
threats. Her main worry was that Grays had become a
major route for human trafficking or 'people smuggling'.
The trade in people, in slaves, is the most lucrative of
all global crimes. Criminal gangs use networks of lorries
to bring in people looking for a better life in the UK.
The journeys may start in China, or Africa, or Eastern
Europe. Often an entire family have raised enough
money to 'send' their young person to England, told
they will be travelling legally, paying thousands of
pounds for what they believe is safe travel, a home in
England and an occupation. And then, if their child
survives the journey, what awaits them here is servitude
and misery. Many of the women are forced into sex
work and others work in our nail bars, the 'best hand
car wash in town' and our bars. They are even working
in plain sight in supermarkets and care homes. The
gang masters will arrange for fake identities, legitimate
National Insurance numbers and a bank account, and

then march their slaves to cash machines to withdraw every penny of that month's salary.

They live in guarded houses of multiple occupancy. More and more in the last five years, I had found myself pulled into support for planning raids on those neighbourhood prisons that are among us in every city. These raids are constantly undertaken by a deployment of police, Border Agency, charities and local authorities. But their purpose is not benign: ultimately they are much more about punitive action and deportation than about humanity.

I am asked for advice because, on paper, the plans for caring for people after disaster also work well for the aftermath of a slavery raid. Often the reception centres for those liberated in Essex or Greater Manchester, Preston or Exeter are modelled on those designed by Disaster Action in the 1990s. There would be a place for a hot shower. A cup of tea. A warm smile. But these are very different places really. Many of the centre users flee by climbing out of the toilet windows into a gang master's waiting car. They are often terrified of the authorities and, in many cases, there are threats being made simultaneously against their family back home to keep them obedient. Others are bound by honour, they believe they have a debt to repay and will bring shame to their families if they flee their bonds. Police colleagues tell me it's not uncommon to have 'freed' the same person four or five times.

The Border Agency regularly stops lorries with suspicious travel patterns or following a tip-off from a fellow driver who could hear voices from within the containers. They were finding them in any port where the lorries could hand over their living cargo. Responders were sometimes getting there with seconds to spare, finding people gasping for air in the back of a lorry that had reached near-fatal temperatures – either too hot or too cold. The men and women inside the lorry are typically travelling only with burner phones and no jewellery or identifying documents, other than little notes from loved ones kept in their underwear. They were taken to local hospitals where they cannot or will not give up their names. I've spoken to the clinicians who examine these men and women first, children and infants too, and were asked to hand things over to the people from the Home Office. Instead, some told me they wrapped the precious letters in tissue and gave them back to the refugee.

The Essex emergency planners and I, along with many other responders, feared that one day we would not get to a lorry in time. And sure enough, on this occasion, they did not. The men and women, some only in their teens, in the Grays lorry had suffered what the judge at the conclusion of a criminal trial would later describe as an excruciatingly painful death. In the back of the lorry, the temperature had been rising along with the carbon dioxide levels, hitting 40C (104F). All the time that the container was at sea. The judge described their desperate attempts to phone the outside world and the damage done to their hands by trying to break through the roof of the container.

Beth wanted to run through her list of first actions with me. At this stage of the response, she would be listening and waiting. Most of the initial actions belong to the police and to the coroner and other agencies tasked with diplomacy and immigration.

I hung up the phone and got my thoughts together before returning to breakfast with Tom, who needed my time now more than ever. I was pumped and focused, like I always am when the calls first come in, but I was also weary. I was tired of watching the risk take shape and then slowly build to an inevitable reality like an abscess. While all the time, the rest of the world knew none of our work or of the harms we were trying to prevent.

My first experience of people smuggling was at the very beginning of my career. Customs and Excise Officers at the Port of Dover stopped a Dutch registered lorry, entering via Zeebrugge. The officers noticed that an external door seal had been cut and found two severely distressed men inside the container and the body of a third. They investigated further and, behind pallets and pallets of tomatoes, found the bodies of fifty-seven more men and women. Of the sixty people trapped as human cargo, only those first two survived.

It was the first debrief I attended as a new Kenyon employee. We were shown photographs of rows and rows of men and women who had been taken to a refrigerated hangar from the lorry, their faces a neon pink from the oxygen starvation and the juice and pith of tomatoes still on their teeth and chin. It was all they had eaten for days. Once the initial media frenzy had calmed, Kent police working jointly with the Metropolitan police had spent over a year trying to find identities for these men and women. The Chinese authorities denied all knowledge of them. In their eyes, the dead's betrayal meant that they simply did not exist.

The police found that some had relatives here already, an older brother, a cousin, working in restaurants and nail bars and car washes, survivors of previous perilous trips. They arranged for them to come and visit their loved ones in a viewing area constructed from a portable cabin and filled with incense sticks and white chrysanthemums. In many Asian countries they are the symbol of death and of funerals. They had asked a Chinese community centre to advise on what was appropriate. I imagined a young copper being sent out to source white chrysanthemums on a Dover high street. Still in uniform, scooping them up from a supermarket bucket or asking a florist to check in the back for any spare bunches.

According to custom, real money also needed to be burned in order to send the deceased on their way. A laborious search ensued for somebody high up in Kent police to sign off the bare minimum of UK taxpayers' money that could be burned in a brazier. Later, Kenyon would carry these various items in a kit marked for 'Chinese deaths'.

A few years later, I was advising the Home Office

Mass Fatalities team when twenty-three men and women trafficked to the UK to pick up cockles on the mudflats of Morecambe Bay in Lancashire were trapped by the incoming tide and drowned. The first 999 calls had come in at 9.13 p.m. on 5 February 2004. The RNLI recovered the first ten bodies and then the next six were recovered by an RAF search and rescue helicopter. The later bodies were washed up days later – all but one that has never been recovered. A further fourteen men and women swam to safety.

We continued to receive regular updates and briefings on incidents like this happening around the country. I learned about 'the snakeheads' who mastermind the journey out of the country and 'the snakes', those who seek a new life in the UK. The entire operation in Morecambe was pervaded by their fear of speaking out, and of huge local penalties for families who tried to assist the investigation back in China. I followed the RNLI investigation as they were dispatched to recover any personal effects – the plastic over-trousers and the cheap wellington boots. They were found on the shoreline for days afterwards; the men and women themselves had been found naked. The force of the sea had ripped their clothes from them.

Beth and I talked again a little later that morning. She sounded tired. There had been one unfortunate error already and the implications were still unfolding. The initial statements to the press had suggested that the deceased were Chinese but it was becoming clear that they were actually from Vietnam. Responders were horrified that this might be interpreted as a lack of due diligence and as a racial slur, that all Asian bodies look the same. In fact, this wasn't a case of racial insensitivity. The documents found with the deceased were false and they laid the trail that the trafficked were Chinese. The responders put two and two together and, for a brief time, came up with five.

As they succumbed to the effects of cerebral anoxia, a lack of oxygen to the brain, the deceased had removed their clothes in an attempt to cool down. In the warehouses, these items had to be checked extremely carefully. Experience had taught us that the trafficked would write identifying details and particularly phone numbers on the inside of their belts and socks and in their trouser hems.

Beth and I moved onto the next steps for her community plan. There was a small Vietnamese community in Grays and there had been some stirring of a response in central London too. There was likely to be fundraising and a vigil.

The responders in Essex were afforded a small, precious number of luxuries in the following hours that are not often available to responders to mass fatalities. The first was the way that the scene was very well contained. All of the deceased had lost their lives in one tight, suffocating space. Usually the police and the scientists have to carefully recover bodies into what is called a 'body holding area' but there was no need for that stage here. The lorry was their coffin and protected them from the newspapers' drones and scavenging wildlife. There were also no families gathering at the scene either. For those human-interest stories, the media looked instead to the villages in Vietnam that the trafficked had called home and left the police to get on with their work.

I signed off by suggesting to Beth that she kept a record of the money she was being asked to spend, which is always a tricky moment on a call. I can tell colleagues find it an uncomfortable segue that I go from white chrysanthemums to who pays in the blink of an eye. But I have seen colleagues held personally liable for the teas and biscuits they have bought for a hundred displaced residents because they could not later produce the receipts. The British have a distaste for raising financial issues at any time and worst of all in times of distress and extremis. This is probably why convention at funerals is still that the undertakers pass out, silently, little brown envelopes of cash or a cheque to the subcontractors and the clergy. I have learned that in the response to mass death, the fights come later and are almost always about who pays the enormous bills left behind. At the time of talking to the emergency planners in Essex, I was also helping two other local authorities unpick massive bills that had been heading their way from police forces, unfairly in my view, after recent emergencies, so I counselled them that it was better to be prepared and wary.

Tom and I made it to the final setting of breakfast. The hotel had a luxurious buffet and I selected thick yoghurt and a granola bursting with syrup-soaked nuts and oats. I stapled a smile on my face and made small talk to a lady next to me, who was desperately trying to keep an impatient toddler quiet as he reached for the little individual portions of hazelnut-chocolate spread. I was grateful that Tom was distracted too, looking out of the window.

For Tom and me, our own personal disaster was by now out of our control. After breakfast, we went out into the hotel's vegetable garden to try to work out our own next steps, but mainly we walked in a foggy, uncomfortable quiet. The smell of thyme was strong. It was the end of the season and while the brassicas and onions had staying power, much of the rest of the garden was spent and starting to retreat back into the soil.

We both kept starting sentences and not finishing them. 'Maybe we could . . .' 'Have you thought about . . .' I had tried calls to action and decisiveness. Recovery listening. Making the best of it. Reading out passages from self-help books. For other responders, I have checklists and plans but for our own crisis the words, the tools, were much harder to find.

In the weeks that followed, Vietnamese authorities worked with Beth and the coroner and the Foreign and Commonwealth Office to make sure that the deceased were returned to the families. They were flown back to the places where their journeys began, the start of the hope and the betrayal. For Beth, it did not matter how they came into her care. She would care for them with the same vigour that I see all the best planners expend on the dead. The public had lost interest by then and because the trial of the lorry driver was now a criminal matter, the law demanded that updates must disappear from the local news broadcast. But behind closed doors, Beth and her colleagues would complete a hundred forms, ensure that the deceased were booked onto flights, that the correct lead lining compatible with international rules on airline cargo has been fitted to the coffins. The first sixteen of the dead were repatriated together. Name plates and papers were checked for any errors ten times.

The Vietnamese government loaned the families the money to pay for the repatriations. Two prices – one for a coffin and a cheaper one if you opted just for the ashes. The families added it to the debts that they continue to pay to the snakeheads. Over that part, Beth and I had no control.

16

The End

We did the planning for the hardest parts of the UK pandemic plan in a cramped room on the top floor of the Cabinet Office building on Great Smith Street in Westminster. Over many years, we fine-tuned the descriptions of the risks and prepared exercise scenarios to test it.

One dirty window ran the length of the room and we had an excellent view of the places where powerful things are done and people like me are often ignored. We met regularly to discuss the nation's most imminent risk: something so likely to happen that it was often described as 'overdue'.[65] Every year, a pandemic was placed at the top of the National Risk Register, the record of the UK's most likely and serious risks, and we would talk about it again.[66] It was exercised at least once a year but without the swagger of the terrorism training. As time went on, we received more and more declined appointments for the exercise from both senior clinicians and government ministers. Perhaps it just wasn't exciting enough.

New fast-track civil servants, fresh from the best university courses in the land, were our handlers. They would fetch us working lunch platters from Prêt à Manger. Our discussions would over-run and the sandwiches would dry out by the radiator. Nobody ate the egg ones.

There was always a point in the pandemic dry runs, the exercises, when it felt like all of the oxygen had left the room. We had no more capacity in our stuffy heads to process the decisions that we were now asking our leaders to make. In the bigger national pandemic exercises, run across every health trust and local council, in much more crowded rooms and with a dial-in conferencing facility for government, the commanders would get bored and frustrated. Each 'inject', an added-in complication, to the scenario was more depressing than the last. They would call 'end ex', the code that meant it was time to go home, and gather around the refreshments, muttering.

The stories imagined in the influenza scenarios were bad enough but we saved more of our angst for the emergent coronas, the MERS, the SARS – acute respiratory diseases that would overwhelm lungs and drown the health service. In 2014, we varied our scenario to include Ebola but that really was too hopeless to play with, with its haemorrhagic symptoms and truly terrible rate of mortality. Pandemic exercises rarely ended with any sense of satisfaction. The Department of Health would lose the recommendations within PowerPoints and jargon-filled reports that would smooth away the urgent human concerns that we were trying to draw attention to. Euphemisms would be deployed to gloss over challenges – for example, the difficulties and risks in moving patients between hospitals and care homes at the peak of an outbreak became 'secondary transfer issues'.

The scenarios imagined in exercises like Cygnus, the biggest pandemic influenza exercise attempted in the UK, were some of the most terror-inspiring I have worked on. The pandemic plan is about broken dreams and losses that build and build. The loss of a loved one, or several loved ones, is the most heartbreaking. But then there are all the other goodbyes that were implicit in the exercise scenarios. The loss of the little café on the corner, the loss of normal rituals, the loss of certainty. There was always hope that the society that would emerge would be stronger and kinder. But there were a few years before you got to that bit. Time without wedding ceremonies or big birthday meals. Months of ten people at a funeral. Years of working hard but with no fun to look forward to at the weekends. As well as the pain of grief for lost loved ones, the other effects of a pandemic would be insidious and most of us would be blind to them at first because there would be no smoking crater or obvious wreckage.

I always felt a pandemic was inevitable, I always felt I would see it in my lifetime because that is what the science told us. But I could also tell that others in the room had bought into the hubris. They had assumed we would stop a pandemic in its tracks.

But, of course, we didn't.

★   ★   ★

I first noticed the signs at the end of December 2019. At every meeting in London people had a cough. My friend texted me on Christmas Day to say she had dragged herself out of bed for a meal that tasted like cardboard and 'this lurgy' seemed to be lingering. I texted back to joke that any minute now Public Health England, the government agency surveilling for health threats globally, would tell us there was something horrible out there.

Suddenly, meetings about 'pandemic planning' were being timetabled in my diary with more urgency from local agencies and the health services[67] but there was nothing happening centrally for us to hook our plans onto. No big announcements from central government, no real scaling up of local resources. As January 2020 wore on, I started to take calls from mortuary managers who were overwhelmed with more deceased than normal. January is traditionally their busiest month and they prepare well for it but this had vastly exceeded their expectations. They rang for a chat, for advice and because they wanted to know if I was hearing it elsewhere, too. The deaths were registered as influenza and bronchopneumonia, they said, but these people had died suddenly or younger. 'The staff are really worried,' one old friend in a mortuary confided, 'and they don't know if the body needs to be ... treated differently. You know, if it's the Wuhan thing.'

The 'Wuhan thing' was eventually confirmed by the World Health Organization: a novel coronavirus had been identified in samples obtained from a cluster of strange pneumonia cases in the Chinese city of Wuhan. The initial analysis of virus genetic sequences suggested that this was the cause of the outbreak. It was, as I had always feared it would be, a coronavirus.[68] The declaration that this was now a global pandemic came on 11 March 2020.

I had long had a special interest in the 2003 SARS outbreak and had hoarded the research articles and commission reports in my growing home library of files and folders. I had a personal connection too. The Kenyon management had sent me out to both Hong Kong and Macau during the outbreak to work with airline clients on their disaster response plans. We mapped the actions that crews would need to take if infected persons started to die on the planes (the plans are still the same now: move the patient to a quiet row and cover them with a blanket). I stood in long airport queues in Hong Kong signing contact tracing forms and having my temperature checked. I checked in to my hotel and followed guidance on reporting any symptoms of respiratory disease. The experience had given me a career-long watchfulness of the corona family of viruses, with their ability to overwhelm the respiratory system and cause complications through-out the body. I fed it into discussions around Exercise Alice, in 2016, which covered a MERS virus outbreak, but once again the commanders called 'end ex' before they had explored all the possibilities.

In February 2020, just as half-term started for the kids, I suddenly felt like I was boiling from the inside and lay on the sofa as usual household chaos raged around me. As I began to shake uncontrollably, Mabel took every coat off the hall coat rack and laid them over me. Cagoules with pockets full of beachcombed gravel and Tom's work blazer that was getting dusty but that I couldn't bring myself to put away. I was violently sick, as I always am, with a temperature and then for several nights in a row, found that I simply could not breathe. I would hiccup for air and nothing would happen. There was still no testing available for Covid-19 and the out-of-hours doctor and my own GP were nervous of naming it as something that theoretically was still so rare in the UK. They diagnosed pneumonia and prescribed strong antibiotics. I slowly got better over the next few weeks, although the virus would leave a nasty tail of severe headaches and fatigue.

One of the many interesting aspects of this novel virus was the way that it was able to mess with our heads, causing a range of cognitive disturbances. A long-lasting 'brain fog', anxiety, loss of concentration and terrible hallucinogenic nightmares. For weeks, I would wake up bathed in sweat and convinced that the house was on fire. One night, I got as far as the front door in an attempt to save my little nephew from an intruder. There was no intruder and my beautiful nephew was hundreds of miles away. I dreamed of burning cities, smoke palling over skyscrapers. Of empty industrial parks with broken windows and packs of feral dogs. And then everything went very still and very clear.

By early March, the calls started to come in on the

hour until 10 or 11 p.m. Almost every colleague, every client, every local authority I had ever worked with wanted to run their plans by me.

Initially the messaging seemed to be that planning for the dead of this type of coronavirus pandemic was unprecedented. The files in the Department of Health and Social Care had little information. But they had not been the government department tasked with readying for this. Planning for the dead of a plague had actually been a well established Home Office work stream, working alongside health colleagues. A work stream that had covered all types of death in disaster, that I had advised on and trained for two decades.

The guidance coming out of central government on how to ready for the dead of pandemic was woefully incomplete. It was confined to a few pages in a PDF concluded by a bizarre diagram for constructing temporary shelving. It looked like the sort of thing that would accompany a flimsy flat-packed wardrobe.

Even worse, government advisers in public health were telling local planners to use the 'IFR', the infection fatality rate, to calculate the local need. But that is not how planning for deaths in a pandemic works. You also need to factor in the other harms: the delayed hospital treatment, the neglected maternal care, the beaten children. The very old or disabled, negative for the virus but unable to access vital care or medication. Then there are the prison riots. The distracted parents. The house fires.

The Department for Health's logistics people asked me to brief a new team that had just won the contract for how to draw up mortuary designs for across the country. As I started to do so, I realised that the contract had been awarded to infrastructure specialists who had never been near a mortuary. I worked particularly hard to re-focus them because I knew that how we cared for our dead now was completely integral to how we came back from this as a nation. There was no room for error. There must never be bodies in corridors or photographed in piles.

Data on the SARS outbreak of 2003 had shown that it had been particularly impactful on patients with diabetes and who were obese. This was likely to lead to many larger bodies. Accommodation for them was a pretty simple omission to spot in a mortuary plan and was a staple of my debriefs prior to the pandemic. We fixed it where we could.

By March 2020, the dead had started to come in much larger numbers. Their endings had many simi-larities to the dead from a thousand other disasters. so many families did not say goodbye in person. The death itself felt sudden and unexpected. Sometimes video calls could be made to a patient but often the families were informed later that they had died. I worry a great deal about the lack of access to a good-bye and the lost ritual of laying eyes on our own dead. This ambiguous loss is one of the most perva-sive and shattering aspects of death in disaster and it lingers. Many hospitals tried to make up memory packs, a handprint from the person in critical care inked onto a poem. I thought a lot about those inky fingers hanging down the side of a white hospital bed, waiting for the end.

The UK prime minister announced the first 'lockdown' in England on 23 March 2020. Strong public health measures were needed but I remembered, in the years before, that we had planned for a much more focused quarantine, with support and resources, and I was alarmed by the closure of so many safe spaces for vulnerable people and children. This felt like the abandonment of those who relied on social care or regular but routine hospital support. I briefed several social work teams in local councils on what we would see next. I suspected that at first we would see nothing at all. In abuse charities and domestic violence helplines the phones went eerily quiet but on the day the first lockdown was lifted they rang at five times their normal volume. That was the first chance some callers had had to escape.

It wasn't something I wanted to be right about. But the data we started to receive in the summer of 2020 showed that during 'lockdown one' there was an increase in paediatric head trauma as the forced invacuation proved the final straw for some carers. Later, domestic violence helpline calls increased by 65 per cent. The admission into hospital of young teens suffering from eating disorders increased by 50 per cent. There was other data too on food and fuel poverty. On the ever-growing hospital waiting lists.

The requests for help I received from government were sporadic and disconnected. I would get calls from the highest offices in Whitehall but there was little appetite for practical, operational advice on what to do. Everything was about 'behavioural insights' teams and how to get the public to comply. There was a huge sense of disappointment if I suggested a different route. The most frequent refrain was 'this will be over soon' and silence when I posited gently that this would take much longer than that. I was also asked not to use the word 'disaster' because this wasn't one.

But all of us emergency planners knew that this would take longer and be more disruptive than was ever sold at the start by our government and indeed many world leaders. It was obvious to us that there would not be a day when it would simply end. Like all disasters, this had changed all those touched by it and would limp on for years.

By the early summer of 2020, I felt that my task was to ready my fellow planners for the time immediately after the first lockdown. It would be then that the true scale of the pandemic would start to reveal itself. I was concerned about the way that it would dissolve the glue of society's fabric. Loss of air travel and the disruption that would cause to the delivery of food, medicines and repatriated bodies. The damage to the National Health Service – years of waiting for a hip operation, calling an ambulance that never comes. The damage to the life chances of thousands of seventeen and eighteen-year-olds. We had listed all this in our planning discussions in Great Smith Street months earlier. But by now those discussions had been reduced to a few paragraphs at the end of reports into COBR and more or less forgotten. Even at the highest levels of briefing, a short, singular 'lockdown' was being sold as a chance for people to re-connect with nature, find love online, boost their skill set, get a puppy.

The truth was that the first lockdown was like a malevolent anaesthetic, pushing the true harms further down the road. Too much time was spent on building the Nightingale hospitals: cavernous warehouses that planners knew we had neither staffing nor equipment to make work. The concept of moving to disaster field operations made sense, but there appeared to be little political will to realise their full potential. Local government planners were spending hours and hours in virtual meetings while NHS responders rebuilt structures that were already in place. Everything was about the virus, rather than the ripple effects of the virus. They were being distracted by the right now but, as a recoverer, I knew that was a siren's voice. There was plenty practically that could be done to make sure that we were a little readier. Extending grant schemes for small businesses and food banks for much longer. Strengthening and supporting local charities. Keeping schools open. There needed to be more thought for recovery in the response.

Because, as we know by now, disasters don't occur in isolation. They domino into other disasters. And, as they unfurl, they become entangled with the other challenges in our lives that would have occurred regardless.

*   *   *

On 16 March, when we'd got back from dropping the children at school, I asked Tom to sit with me for a while. We had been struggling on for months. He had finally been diagnosed with an atypical type of Ménière's disease, an incurable condition that affects the inner ear, and in his case affected every aspect of his life. He had also lost his right-sided hearing completely and his balance; high-pitched tinnitus and terrible headaches blighted most days. We now knew definitively that he would never be allowed to fly again. I tried to interest him in a future but all he wanted was the life before and there was no in-between. The only time he would leave the house was to take the children to school and to run and run and run – marathon distances almost daily until sometimes he was sick in the hedgerow.

And now what felt like a mini-disaster for our family had a new backdrop in the shape of the pandemic. In March 2020, much of the public appeared to have succumbed to 'the *Skyfall* effect' and seemed to be hopeful that this was just a brief blip. I was worried that Tom might be thinking like that too, that a few weeks of an enforced quarantine would be enough to see this thing off.[69] That sophisticated teams of health professionals would get a handle on it and then he could go back to his own disaster. In moments of complete clarity, in the middle of the night, I had real-ised that unless he and I were able to see this thing in the same way, our relationship would not survive it. I needed him to be prepared. I needed his engagement and support. I needed him.

I pushed a mug of tea across to him. I thought carefully about what to say. Tom is a man who likes briefings and shies away from emotional outbursts. I lowered my voice – volume and tone – and said quietly, 'I know what this is. I need you to listen to me.'

This was not a lockdown of six weeks. This was life now, for a very long time.

Where there is doubt, there is no doubt.

He nodded slowly. 'I believe you,' he said.

Often the best emergency response, in the long term, is done at the local level. And so the other meeting I arranged in the second week of March 2020 was at my children's school with the governors and village leaders. I told them that because our village was a farming community they would likely be designated as 'key workers'. I told them that this would not be gone in six weeks but instead would probably define the rest of their working lives. They knew me only as the mum at the school gates with the two little girls but they took what I said on board. ('I've checked and she is who she says she is!' said the headmaster to everyone, helpfully.) We set up a village response group, which was almost exclusively staffed by already over-burdened mothers, which did extra shopping for our elderly. Jay pitched in and ferried prescriptions to the sheltered accommodation at the heart of the village and Marks and Spencer brie to the shielding patriarchs. Our district councillor caught on quickly and donated his salary to a 'war fund' for anyone in need and bought mobile phones so that a number could be put out for people who needed help.

The village in Nottinghamshire where we had begun to raise our girls relied heavily on agriculture for its income. Our strawberries and raspberries can be found in every 'finest' range in the country's supermarkets and I told the farmers they should do everything they could to ready themselves for a busy few months because of increased demand for UK-grown food as borders closed. Jay and I also tried to tackle a darker local secret. At the back of our houses loom polytunnels forcing the fruit on almost all year round and behind the polytunnels are tens of shabby caravans where many workers live, employed to pick the fruit. They are not included in the numbers of residents or any census of its needs. Jay ferried food orders to them and made it very clear, to them and to their handlers, that we were watching out for them.

And this was Elizabeth and Mabel's disaster, too. I had spent the last five years as an adviser on a Save the Children and Lancaster University project about children's resilience in disaster and the thing I most wanted for my girls was that they would not only survive this but be even stronger. There is a scene at the end of the film *Hook* that always makes me cry. Robin Williams as grown-up Peter Pan is counselling the smallest of the Lost Boys, now that he is leaving Neverland. Peter instructs them, 'I want you to take care of everything that's smaller than you.' The littlest Lost Boy, Too Small, asks, 'Then who do I look after?' 'Neverbugs – the little ones,' says Peter, before flying off, back home to London.

I knew I could get my girls through it if they had Neverbugs to look after. If they looked outwards, if they had jobs and roles and people to care for. So they made signs and posters. We ran sunflower growing and fancy dress 'front garden' competitions. Parcels for newborn babies. Doorstep visits with cake and fruit. Other parents in the village and on Facebook got involved and pretty soon we had a children's army.

Very slowly, Tom found horizons to swim towards, too. There were many days when it was best to leave him to sleep in a chair but on others he tended our garden and started a vegetable patch, and slowly his interest in life within a pandemic grew. He book-marked articles for me on food shortages and vaccine developments. We started to laugh a lot more again. Having to wear a mask made lip-reading difficult and we would chuckle at his attempts to understand super-market workers. I persuaded him to buy a fancy hear-ing aid with a phone app. I remembered Alan's teach-ings from another lifetime. Grief is best dealt with in the tiniest of incremental steps: how about you make the cup of tea today? Shall we walk to the end of the drive? Let's redecorate the kitchen . . .

One day, I hung up his framed certificates and his Huffman Aviation baseball cap in our front hall. Under the pretext of researching for this book, I asked him to get his denim blue logbook out from a dusty drawer, unopened for two years. The most precious thing a pilot owns is this handwritten record of every flight ever taken. But he was able to check on some of the first dates, to check the name of the plane. The Diamond DA20 Katana. To remember and to commemorate.

Right now, I am still very much inside many recoveries. As time has gone on, the idea of how we come back from the pandemic has become more prioritised in governmental and corporate minds. Each week, there is more acceptance that disasters from other times and places have something to teach us. There is more interest in how to flick switches in public minds from response to recovery. There is also a realisation that some aspects of the disaster fade while others linger for much longer.

I have been advising on much more heartening and life-affirming work – strategies for supporting children and for building more resilient hospitals and mortuaries. A number of studies that will re think the way we care for older people in the new world we build. I try to stay hopeful that these will, for once, be grown with proper roots so they are not easily swept away this time.

We are all disaster survivors now. The legacy of this particular catastrophe will be long-lasting: we will feel the effects of Covid-19 for many years to come. Other generations after us will speculate and ruminate on it, as we did about the ones that came before. I had often wondered about how people kept going in long and chronic events like the Blitz of the Second World War and now I realise that it was only afterwards that this period was framed neatly and bookended with a beginning and an end. At the time, you just kept putting one foot in front of the other, each time that dawn broke.

For me, one of the most troubling aspects of the point that we have reached is that our response has been so anti-human. The government's response to the Covid-19 pandemic has included hefty doses of fear in the messaging. People are afraid – of the virus but worse, of each other. More people started to die at home without seeking help for other medical emergencies than of the virus.

Just like with chemical and nuclear threats, fear is a dark genie that is not easy to recapture into its bottle. Its effects will linger long after the disease itself has felt more under control. The place that we find ourselves is spectrum-opposite from that on which a healthy recovery is built. We and our children have been framed as vectors of disease. I wish we could have found a way to have kept shame, stigma and threat out of public health messages. I hope that soon, we can find a way to reach back to each other again, without the fear.

The recovery graph that I draw for my colleagues to work to has a rollercoaster of peaks and troughs that stretches into the next few years. Our mood has been lifted and lowered by new school terms and changing seasons, the ending of economic buffers, the highs of major sporting events and then the crashing lows of family after family suffering bereavements.

Historically, as a pandemic wanes, the pogroms and the rioting begins. Whether we follow that path is up to us. We have never been on more of a knife-edge than we are now. My soul hopes for the best – and has an expansive frame of reference to draw on to feel hopeful. It is both my nature and my life's work to believe we can clear ourselves out of the thickets of disaster and then begin the labour of healing. But my professional experience has also taught me that there are many bumps ahead and that we have to be painfully honest about those. All the planners can do now is be the light-bearers, illuminating the traps and helping as many as they can to navigate the next steps.

AFTERWORD
The Beginning

'Disaster sometimes knocks down institutions and structures and suspends private life, leaving a broader view of what lies beyond. The task before us is to recognize the possibilities visible through that gateway and endeavour to bring them into the realm of the everyday.'

A Paradise Built in Hell, Rebecca Solnit

This is a different book to what it would have been without the pandemic. The longing for a life before is something we're now all familiar with. The rebuild this time is global. We are all looking through the gateway and though they may be hard to discern, there are possibilities beyond. Those possibilities are far from equal or level but this will be a disaster recovery that involves us all.

I'm often asked what we should learn from all of this. History suggests that for a time, the lessons, the impetus from the pandemic will be vivid – like new scars – and it will seem anathema to those who lived through it that they would ever be forgotten. But the pace of life, finite memory and the necessary forgetting of those who hold political power will ensure that many of them are lost. That is the true contradiction of living through disaster – you catch glimpses of the very best and very worst of life before all is softened to somewhere in between.

What matters more perhaps are the lessons we take from all this at an individual level. The most important thing now is to look after each other. Start with those closest to you and work outwards. Find a balance between the negative stresses of a life in readiness and fear and the comfort of 'being prepared'.

Disasters of any kind are hardest on those already struggling. There are many reasons to be hopeful about the way that communities have connected more closely, little by little, and often enabled by technological solutions. I would like to see community readiness as a tenet of school education and night classes and more support for people to get involved with scouting, volunteering and citizenship programmes.

There is much to be angry about. But now I try not to spend too much time feeling angry with those in power or losing sleep about the trust in them we have lost. In the pandemic, we all saw behind the (threadbare) curtains; we saw the truth of emergency planning and understood that there is no slick command room or James Bond. But we saw also that where it matters, at local level, the planners and responders rose to the challenge. And that we ourselves have more resilience than we knew.

When I was young, I heard the words 'Somebody ought to sort this' and took it as a directive. If I could speak to that little girl now I would tell her that she could not sort it all but that the quest in itself had a point. That every tiny little help she brought had purpose. That there is value in a warm drink and a reassuring smile at the worst time of somebody else's life. I would tell her about the importance of resting the dead, the significance of a chance to say goodbye and the nature of the death itself. About the value we may place on the fragments of a loved one and also on the things that travel with them. That there can be sacred importance in ceramic elephants. That working with the dead does not need to cause lasting damage to those who care for them if responders are cared for and supported properly.

I would show her that the longing for a place gone, *hiraeth*, is worthy of respect in a hierarchy of losses. That in disaster there are sharp hurts and long, drawn-out chronic pains. And that these pains have names from other places that don't always fit into modern framings of mental health. That disasters are political and entangled with power, and that pointing out that things are going wrong will sometimes make her incredibly unpopular.

I would also tell her to get outside more, swim more, feel the sun and learn how to slow down her racing brain. To learn that there are moments to step forward and moments to wait.

I would tell her that she will take a lot of flak for her optimism, for her enthusiasm to understand more about what comes after disaster but also that there is no greater time to see the potential for rebuild and opportunity than in the aftermath.

I would tell her to keep going, to hold on for those moments, because there will always be disasters and there will always be people who want to help. There will always be hurting and there will always be a rebuild.

Those of us who work in disaster will never stop scanning the stars to see what they have in store for us next. Or finding ways to help people put their lives back together in the aftermath. But I have learned, or, at least, I am learning, to make room for other moments too.

I reach for my phone after it beeps a text notification. It alerts me that a parcel has arrived of books and art materials for the children's charity that nestles at the base of the Grenfell Tower. I look out at the view from my kitchen window: sunshine, bird tables, chewed dog toys and kids' tricycles.

Tom sets a cup of tea among my papers and smiles. 'What next?' he asks

Acknowledgements

I have been supported by a cast of literally thousands of wonderful people in my life. All of those hands that have held me up, and the smiles and the snacks that have sustained me. Only a fraction of you can be mentioned in the text but you are all weaved in there. Thank you is not enough for any of you.

There are also a few people I did not get to tell in time that this book would not exist without them. The loss of one of my most important influences, the TV producer and investigative journalist Katy Jones in 2015, inspired me to find ways to bring the stories of disaster out into the world. This book is fuelled by her and her methods. Eternal gratitude to her dear friend Saskia Abbot who persuaded me not to wear a body camera, but to instead try and write as much as I could down on paper. Equally this book would also not exist without my friend, mentor and travel companion Eve Coles, who died shortly before its completion. Love always to her and the entire Coles Clan.

My emergency planners, you have literally been the wind beneath my wings. No longer Cinderellas, my dear friends – we are making a musical! We have faced a tough and relentless series of tests and we all know there will be many more. A special shout out to my pandemic crew who got me through our latest challenges, and to Aimee who is the very best of us. I also want to thank the members of the Association of Anatomical Pathology Technology, who I will champion and fangirl until the end of time.

Thank you to all those communities of disaster who have let me in. I owe a particularly large debt to the people of North Kensington, London and the people of Toll Bar, Doncaster. Both places have been subjected to nightmares, but are also exemplars of humanity, compassion and perseverance. I am also indebted to Dr Renée Kosalka and the Coroners of Québec for the access they gave me to the aftermath of the Lac Mégantic disaster.

To the members of the incredible organisation that is Disaster Action, thank you from the bottom of my heart for letting me watch and learn. During the pandemic, you lost one of our figureheads and the bravest woman I have ever met, Dr Maureen Kavanagh. Thank you my darling Maureen, for teaching me the purest meaning of mother's love, and all of the lioness's fight that goes with that.

I have been privileged to receive guidance from the best of mentors. I want to particularly thank: Alan Puxley, Dr Anne Eyre, Jelena Watkins, Pam Dix, Sophie Tarrasenko, Retired Detective Jen Williams, Dr Lesley Perman-Kerr, Professor Phil Scraton, Jimmy McGovern, Debbie Brooker-Evans, Bernadette

Duncan, Cheryl Wells, Adewale Adesina, Professor Caroline McMullan, Professor Alexander McFarlane, Dr Grady Bray, Robert Rowntree, Gail Rowntree, Professor Catherine Mason, Dr James Adeley, Heidi Rana, Andre Rebello, Alison Thompson, Derek Winter, Clive Brooks, Steve Gregory, Simon Taylor, the late great Graham Walker, Peter Stevenson, Susan Greenwood, Michael Greenwood, Dr Mark Roberts, Dr Meredith Tise, Professor Jenny Edkins, Professor John Troyer, Dr Kate Woodthorpe, Dr Brenda Mackie, Dr Philip Marsden, Dr John Robson, Alison Anderson, John Pitchers, Susan Rudnik, Lucy Knight, Debbie Brooker-Evans, Melissa Brackley, Dr Danielle Osborn, Jacqui Semple, Jeannie Barr, Matt Hogan, Helen Hinds, Ewan Phillips, Pat Hagan, Dr Lisa Wood, Professor Maggie Mort, Nigel Humphries, Emma Dodgson, Rebecca Pritchett, Dr Elspeth Van Veeren, Dr Hugh Deeming, Dr Aimee Mundorff, Professor Dawnie Steadman, Professor Lori Peek, Professor Lucina Hackman, Professor Dame Sue Black and the Detectives from the Special Command Unit charged with the return of personal effects at the Metropolitan Police 2005–2008.

To my fellow co-founders of the After Disaster Network, University of Durham – we picked an apposite time to try and save the world.

To Jen and Alex Forrest and Nellie of course. Watching your strength gave me the strength to finish this.

To my beloved Jay and all of his clan. Not enough words in the universe.

Thank you Emma Stanley, the Bradleys, the Elliotts, Jean Brown, Kerry Driver, the Morgans, the Wilkinsons, Katy Medley and Richard and Yvette for the village life support.

Medically, there is only one reason I have stayed relatively upright through the various shenanigans in this book and that is via the care of an excellent gynaecologist, Miss Maisa Salman. I owe my babies to the medical legend that is Professor Munter Khamashta. I also want to pay tribute to the staff of the Emergency Department, Doncaster Royal Infirmary who saved my husband's life.

I could not have wished for a better home for my tales than Hodder and Stoughton. Thank you Kirty Topiwala for believing in these stories and for making them into something that could travel into the world. My thanks also to Anna Baty, Cameron Myers, Rebecca Mundy, Sahina Bibi and Al Oliver.

I owe a debt too big to ever repay to the word-wizard that is Celia Hayley. You were the most patient person I have ever met. Thank you for letting me barter your precise cogency and wisdom for my pandemic survival advice. Thank you too to Chris Morris for making each draft better. Thank you to Cathy Rentzenbrink for the exceptional memoir training.

There have been many quirky twists of the fates, and sprinklings of lady luck, in my life but none greater than meeting the best literary agent in the world, Jo Unwin. Thank you Jo. Also my infinite gratitude to the most perfectly formed team in the world ever at JULA: Milly Reilly, Rachel Mann and

Nisha Bailey. Donna Greaves, an extra thanks for the confidence and the encouragement to finish this.

Finally, to my family… Sam, Erin, Megan, Jude and Emma – four different time zones but always together. Thank you always to Gran Lucy, Nanny Pat, the Rogersons, Davis', Simons, Singletons, Taylors, Handys, Wilsons, Hills, Myers, Chaplins, Levitts, Paynes, Redmans, Hughes', Tolmans, Wrights and Steeles. The Griffiths, Sweets, Hunts and Lewis'. Beccy, Jane, Lou, Sal, and their clans, Mike R, Frank H, the Cambridge Girls and the Wallasey Girls.

Nick and Kate Easthope – thank you for everything.

Mum and Dad – you are everywhere in this book but behind the scenes, probably with some digestives and a kettle on, just how you like it. People ask me, how do you do this? Because of you.

To my precious, perfect Elizabeth and Mabel – in terms of the logistics of actually writing this book you were no help at all, but what would be the point of writing it without you? You are my reason and my horizon. I am so glad that you clung on my strongest Titans. I love you moon and back. One life, my beautiful warriors, live it.

To Tom – I have fallen in love many times during the timeline of this book, always with you. It is you that gave me the strength and the confidence to pursue my path and through your steadfastness the world has been changed. You are the scaffold around this family. You are enough.

Endnotes

1. New Zealand Red Cross *Leading in Disaster Recovery: A Companion Through the Chaos* guidance developed after the New Zealand earthquakes of 2010 and 2011. This can be downloaded here: https://www.preventionweb.net/publication/leading-disaster-recovery-companion-through-chaos.
2. Totemic events are often shortened to their place names or dates which can seem a cruel shorthand. I have used their dates or place names here for clarity.
3. Funeral directors often bid for a local coroners' contract and one way to win it is to have enough shiny, black ambulances to be able to respond to a small disaster like this.
4. For a full exposition of these events see Scraton, P. (1999; reissued 2009 and 2016), *Hillsborough. The Truth*, Mainstream Publishing.
5. In Lord Taylor's public inquiry one year after the disaster and, more forcefully, in the Hillsborough Independent Panel report of 2012. The gate had been opened, not forced, as the result of a terrible error by South Yorkshire Police and match commander David Duckenfield. In 2016, an inquest verdict confirmed that fans had been unlawfully killed.
6. Weir, A. (2000) *The Tombstone Imperative*, Pocket Books.
7. In Scotland, there are slight differences to the role and their equivalent of a coroner is a procurator fiscal. Northern Ireland also has a coronial system.
8. Phil went on to track down every statement available to him and his book, *The Truth*, is his account of this. He went

on to become the lead author of the Hillsborough Independent Panel Report, which fundamentally changed perceptions of the disaster and rewrote the truth for all to know. But that was in the future.

9. 'What is a disaster?' both as a question about severity of effects and metrics and also in a deeper philosophical sense is a key question in the field of emergency planning and response. Whole texts and conferences are devoted to it. Many of the events described in this book would be categorised as emergencies or major incidents, although both tsunamis would certainly be considered as much more impactful. In the UK, we tend to base definitions around events that are outside the normal and overwhelm standard resources. For a recent and highly detailed discussion of categorising events into emergency, disaster and catastrophe see: Montano, S. (2021), *Disasterology: Dispatches from the Frontlines of the Climate Crisis*, Park Row.

10. The decade from the late 1980s into the early 1990s saw major mass fatality incidents almost every year, with sometimes just a few weeks in between them. For a full list of UK disasters and their legal consequences on the families in the 1990s see: Eyre, A. and Dix, P. (2010), *Collective Conviction*, Liverpool University Press.

11. The full National Commission report is available at https://9-11commission.gov/report/

12. The business model for the four or five commercial disaster management teams that exist globally is not to spend money on salaried staff but to have a small number of managers in the office and then a team of willing retained colleagues.

13. Asbestos levels were forty-seven times higher than international safety limits. A lawyer acting for the families described the Ground Zero disaster site as 'the most toxic site ever'.

14. Mark Petrocelli's family were first notified of a DNA match on 25 September 2001.

15. There are a number of verdicts available to a coroner as a cause of death, including unlawful killing, misadventure, accidental, suicide or open. They may also provide a detailed narrative verdict with the 'story' of what happened but no clear decision or verdict.

16. The body of interpreter Hussein Osman was found later. The body of cameraman Fred Nerac has never been found.

17. The Civil Contingencies Act 2004 that would place planning and responding for national and international incidents on a formal, statutory footing was only then heading through Parliament.

18. Eighty-eight Australians died in the attack.

19. An accurate death toll of the event is disputed. It is feared that the number is underestimated and does not include many undocumented migrant workers.

20. Visual identification for the purposes of identification can be problematic. But this is not the same as the family viewing the body for therapeutic purposes, which is something I have fought to protect.

21. What were originally called 'unique medical identifiers' like metal hip joints proved to be problematic once there was a trade in recycled joints. The register of breast implant numbers was closed in the early 2000s in the UK, so these can also be hard to identify forensically.

22. Although the death toll spoken of publicly for a suicide bombing usually deducts the bombers themselves, they are also cared for in death and have bodies and more usually body parts or fragments that must be identified and examined. Often now they are taken to a separate place but for 7 July, a separate area was built for them as an offshoot of the main mortuary structure.

23. They were previously known as 'family assistance centres' but this was changed to avoid any sense of alienation or exclusion to partners or friends.

24. The social science theory that partially explains the issues behind this dissonance is called 'the Certainty Trough' and was first described by Donald MacKenzie writing about how people who work with nuclear weapons often have much less faith in the science that they see up close, than people on the outside.

25. With all incidents, as coins and bank notes that are separated from the wallet are not easily identifiable to an individual, these are gathered together and returned to banks who then donate the total amount to the disaster fund.

26. Yi-Fu Tuan first described the personal effects after disaster as 'a magpie hoard of touch and heart' and it has stuck with me ever since. Tuan, Y. (1977), *Space and Place*, Minneapolis: University of Minnesota Press.
27. Concepts of lifescapes are used in disasterology, anthropology and geography to map out how communities use and interact with resources such as community centres and schools. The places and spaces are entangled with the social identities of residents and are integral to the community fabric.
28. We use 'remediation' a lot in emergency planning and response to mean putting back together and fixing the broken structures or cleaning up contamination.
29. Kai Erikson is a world authority on writing about the effects of catastrophic events on societies. These include books on nuclear fallout and life after fatal floods in Buffalo Creek, USA, in 1972.
30. The video can be viewed here: https://www.youtube.com/watch?v=-z3mBIi084Q
31. Rendezvous point; Strategic Co-ordinating Group and Scientific Advisory Group in Emergencies.
32. Blakemore, E., 'The Chernobyl Disaster: What happened and the long-term impacts', *National Geographic*, 17 May 2019. Available at https://www.nationalgeographic.com/culture/article/chernobyl-disaster
33. It is popularly, but not officially, referred to as COBRA: those 'in the know' never use the A.
34. The full acronym stands for chemical, biological, radiological and nuclear and then the E is for 'high yield explosives' – high energy detonations – which are designed to create large numbers of casualties.
35. Created by local professional photographer Claude Grenier.
36. At almost the exact time of night, six months later, on 23 January 2014, thirty-two older people were killed in a fire within a residential home in the Québec town of L'Isle Verte. The two forensic operations had many similar features and the same responders deployed again.
37. I interviewed the coroners, the anthropologist, the pathologists, the police detectives and the DNA scientists who worked on Lac-Mégantic as part of my research.

38. The video can be viewed here: https://www.youtube.com/watch?v=9eBwDzJm7_0

39. The fates dealt Malaysia Air a particularly cruel blow. Their management, their emergency planners and their family assistance teams had already spent 2014 dealing with the aftermath of the loss of another of their planes, MH370 in March. Only parts of the wreckage have ever been found but accident investigators work on the theory that the captain deliberately veered off course and flew the plane into the ocean.

40. For further information see Stadler, N. (2006) 'Terror, corpse symbolism, and taboo violation: the "Haredi Disaster Victim Identification Team in Israel" (Zaka)' *Journal of the Royal Anthropological Institute*, (N.S.) 12, 837–58.

41. The Netherlands appeared to be a more neutral choice, which the Russians accepted, more than say the USA or the UK. It also made pragmatic sense as the greatest proportion of the deceased were from the Netherlands. A large facility was built to Interpol guidelines, with substantial UK input.

42. We tip our hat to this today when we use the term 'gutted' to describe ourselves as disappointed.

43. Also known as Crew Resource Management.

44. Maines, Rachel. P. (1999), *The Technology of Orgasm: 'Hysteria', the Vibrator and Women's Sexual Satisfaction*, The John Hopkins University Press, p 23.

45. This is why planners need to have a little bit of expertise on just about everything!

46. This particular compound risk was a theme of a conference keynote talk that I gave to Irish government emergency planners in the spring of 2019. It was a 'super forecast' of what was to come next and I am pleased that it was recorded for posterity online. A summary can be found here https://business.dcu.ie/emii-research-symposium-critical-thinkers-in-emergency-management-research-an-international-perspective/

47. It is generally harder to garner support and funding for exercises for floods, pandemics and other scenarios that test the humans more than the kit. Terrorism and aviation disasters tend to be the most popular.

48. The 'Joint Emergency Services Interoperability Programme' was an approach to support the better integration of the emergency services at the scene of the incident. It was born out of a failing identified in the 7/7 attacks and is under review after a number of recent incidents where interoperability once again struggled.

49. On the evening of 13 November 2015, gunmen linked to Islamic extremism opened fire and used bombs in a Paris concert hall killing ninety people and injuring many others. A further forty people were killed in a nearby stadium, restaurant and bars.

50. Many news organisations will now broadcast the rumoured names, speculated on locally and on social media, as if proven. The police cannot ever compete with this and it is now a common phenomenon for families to find out about their loved ones' involvement through media sources.

51. There are also now many examples of family members finding out about their loved ones' potential involvement in an incident through smartphone technology. This does not confirm death or even identity but will often be the first sign now that something has happened. An early, widely reported case was that of Bob Weiss, who used an Apple app to try to locate his daughter Veronica in 2012. He'd heard reports of a shooting at her university campus. When he used the locator function on the app it showed she was at one of the three crime scenes. I would say this is now a common feature of major incident and crimes. Families are using the apps and rushing to the scene of incidents like stabbings and road collisions long before the police can notify them.

52. Recently, someone ordering equipment misheard and ordered 100 clocks rather than the protective footwear 'clogs' that mortuary staff use.

53. In 2016, five men from Ghana were killed when they were crushed by a wall collapse at a Birmingham metal recycling plant. Many of the debrief points from the local police force centred on their challenges when communicating with families, and particularly the fact that some English and Latin terms don't translate easily – e.g., next of kin and ante-mortem.

54. In order to get the DNA necessary to test, bones and teeth are often ground down and destroyed in the process. So you may be able to provide some answers but no actual remains to bury.

55. Okri, B. (2019) writing in *After Grenfell: Violence, Resistance and Response*. Edited by Bulley, D., Edkins, J. and El -Enany, N. Pluto Press.

56. A detailed analysis of the effects of the cladding and also the composition of the window frames, as well as further discussion of the technical failings, can be found in Kernick, G. (2021), *Catastrophe and Systemic Change: Learning from the Grenfell Tower Disaster and Other Fires*, London Publishing Partnership. A timeline of events is here: www.bbc.co.uk/news/uk-40301289. Information on the ongoing public inquiry is available here: www. grenfelltowerinquiry.org.uk

57. As the baby, Logan Gomes, died before he was born, he cannot have his own inquest or legal proceedings, but his death has been described as 'highly relevant to inquest proceedings' in a declaration by HM coroner in September 2018. The coroner appointed to the Grenfell disaster was also the coroner for Exercise Unified Response.

58. Plans had envisaged that in an incident of this scale, family liaison detectives trained in Disaster Victim Identification would be released from other police forces. A request was made but the mutual aid was not available.

59. There is a long history of unidentified remains of those who have never been formally reported missing in disaster. They often remain within the mortuary facilities and many from 9/11 are still cared for in the New York laboratories. Whole bodies, who simply do not match any register or ante-mortem yellow form. At the start of my DVI career, the final deceased male from the 1987 King's Cross fire was discovered to be Alexander Fallon. He was not identified for sixteen years and his remains were interred in an unmarked grave. Scotland Yard tried many avenues to identify him, even consulting a Spanish medium. The scientists at the time had estimated his age at between fifty and sixty but in fact he was seventy-two when the fire claimed him, although a facial reconstruction that was attempted was found to be very accurate once his identity

became known. Alexander Fallon had been living on the edge of society for some time before the fire and had not immediately been reported missing.

60. Almost all larger-scale disasters in recent times have a disputed death toll. The published figure of those dead in the Indian Ocean tsunami, for example, is believed to substantially underestimate (perhaps for political reasons) the amount of undocumented migrant workers killed. Some incidents like air crashes have more defined 'manifests' – lists of passengers – but even then there can be mistakes, fraud or sometimes an extra deceased as a repatriated coffin in the hold. After a Boeing 747 cargo flight operated by the airline El Al crashed into a tower block in Bijlmermeer, Amsterdam, in 1992, there were many years of contention over the final death toll. Concerns were raised that a number of undocumented migrants were missing from it.

61. The local council has been condemned for both their treatment of residents before and during the fire but also the oversight of the refurbishment process itself in the years before the fire. They are named defendants in ongoing civil litigation as well as being under investigation by the Metropolitan police. In 2017 the Metropolitan police announced, 'After an initial assessment of that information, the officer leading the investigation has today notified Royal Borough of Kensington and Chelsea and the Kensington and Chelsea Tenant Management Organisation that there are reasonable grounds to suspect that each organisation may have committed the offence of corporate manslaughter, under the Corporate Manslaughter and Corporate Homicide Act 2007.'

62. It is not just Doncaster. Caravan parks used to keep communities together are a regular feature in US disaster response and temporary lodges, large caravans, were also used in Christchurch after the earthquakes.

63. NHS data released 6 months after the fire showed over 200 diagnoses of PTSD in children from the tower and the surrounding areas.

64. Some local councils continued to place great weight on their emergency planning and readiness, scraping bits of budgets from somewhere else to ensure there was still a

training day or enough in a bank account to buy tea and coffee in a rest centre. I ran courses on emergency planning for their housing staff and on the key principles of emergency planning and disaster victim identification for their social workers. The best local authorities don't wait for public inquiry reports – often ten years in the works – to make their own improvements and build a team ready for the next time. Unlike other councils, who had become weary or complacent, the councils in the county of Essex are known for regularly training their housing teams and their social workers for a range of occurrences.

65. It was 'scored' on the risk register from 2004 onwards as being extremely likely in the next five years – disease outbreak is one of the most common and re-occurring threats that humanity faces. By 2020, it was considered long overdue as something we would face.

66. The highest national risk was termed as an influenza pandemic but in terms of the effects on society, in my experience we regularly gave consideration to this being a coronavirus-related pandemic and exercised for both. There was ultimately little difference in the losses to society that repeated waves of either would cause.

67. These were being organised by Local Resilience Forums: a non-legal entity that brings together the responding agencies in a geographical region.

68. The virus is referred to as SARS-CoV-2 and the associated disease as Covid-19.

69. 'Lockdowns' in emergency planning, prior to the pandemic, referred only to the locking in of people during a marauding terror incident or shooting. Its use here was not detailed in the prior plans, although the use of quarantining and some requirement to stay at home was. It had been expected that the government would use powers under the Civil Contingencies Act, 2004 to do this. Instead, they introduced entirely new legislation. One reason for this may be that the CCA powers require much greater and more regular scrutiny by Parliament than the Coronavirus Act, 2020.

An invitation from the publisher

Join us at www.hodder.co.uk, or follow us
on Twitter @hodderbooks to be a part of
our community of people who love the very
best in books and reading.

Whether you want to discover more about a book
or an author, watch trailers and interviews, have the
chance to win early limited editions, or simply browse
our expert readers' selection of the very best books,
we think you'll find what you're looking for.

And if you don't, that's the place to tell us what's missing.

We love what we do, and we'd love you to be a part of it.

www.hodder.co.uk

 @hodderbooks

 HodderBooks

HodderBooks